Stalked by Socialism

Stalked by Socialism

An Escapee From Communism Shows How We're Sliding Into Socialism

Jana Kandlova
aka Jane Benson

STALKED BY SOCIALISM
AN ESCAPEE FROM COMMUNISM SHOWS HOW WE'RE SLIDING INTO SOCIALISM

iUniverse books may be ordered through booksellers or by contacting:

iUniverse
1663 Liberty Drive
Bloomington, IN 47403
www.iuniverse.com
1-800-Authors (1-800-288-4677)

ISBN: 978-1-6632-0238-3 (sc)
ISBN: 978-1-6632-0434-9 (hc)
ISBN: 978-1-6632-0239-0 (e)

Library of Congress Control Number: 2020910101

Print information available on the last page.

iUniverse rev. date: 06/25/2020

Contents

Foreword

by Jim Vicevich

During my 43 years on television and radio, most recently as the host of "Sound Off Connecticut," I've consistently spoken out against bloated, busybody government. I've encouraged my listeners to call in with stories of how the government has trampled on their rights. And I've interviewed a lot of very smart people who have explained how the government has spent decades worming its way into our lives and eating away at our liberty.

All of them have had a lot to say, but none have said it quite like Jane Benson does in this book.

Jane, who was born and raised in communist Czechoslovakia, knows firsthand what happens when the government becomes too powerful. She knows how the government takes its control over the economy, health care, jobs, and more, and turns it into control over your life. She knows how the glowing promises the government makes somehow never come to be, and instead are replaced by threats. And she knows how much people can suffer when they speak out against a government that has grown too powerful.

She knows all of these things, and now she's sounding a warning to all Americans.

Jane begins with a brief sketch of her life in what she sarcastically refers to as "commie paradise." Czechoslovakia was such a "wonderful" place that she fled the country when she was just 19, back in 1988, knowing she would never be able to see her family again, and they, in turn, would be punished by the government for "allowing" her to leave.

Jane loved the freedom she could practically smell when she arrived in the U.S., but after a while, she began to notice certain signs of socialism. Small things that most people don't notice, but definitely signs that America was slowly sliding toward a more socialistic society. She saw that we have become accustomed to running to the government for help whenever trouble strikes, not realizing that even if the help is effective, it always costs us a bit of our freedom. She saw that we've gotten used to a government that has grown so big that no one really knows how many laws and regulations it's imposing on us. And she saw that many of us have forgotten what it means to be truly free, to live the way we choose to.

On my radio show and now on my podcast, RadioViceOnLine.com, I've been calling for smaller, leaner, less intrusive government for years.

This book does the same, and convincingly so. **Stalked By Socialism** speaks with a power and urgency that only a person who has lived under a genuinely socialist government can truly understand.

Note to the Readers on Communism and Socialism

Throughout this book, I use the words communism and socialism interchangeably. I understand that there are differences between the two, and socialism is often thought of as a step on the way to communism. I also know that countries that call themselves socialist are really communist. However, communism and socialism are, in their real-world application, nearly indistinguishable, which is why I treat them as being one and the same in this book.

Disclaimer

This book presents important moments in my life, to the best of my recollection. The information about Communist Czechoslovakia and communism in general is not meant to be textbook history. There may be errors in dates and motivations, for what I have described is based on what I experienced and learned in communist-run public schools, coupled with information and opinions picked up from my parents and grandparents.

Chapter One

Beginnings

July 4, 1988 lives in my memory as if it happened yesterday. I was standing at a boarding gate at Václav Havel Airport Prague, watching through a window as a plane taxied slowly toward me, its engines screaming and kicking up their own private wind storm. I was 19 years old, nervously waiting for the plane (could it be this one?) that would sweep me off to the United States to my boyfriend, David. My mother, sister, and a childhood friend were waiting with me, and when I looked over at them, I could see they were already wiping away tears. That's because all of us knew I wasn't really taking a vacation; I was leaving Czechoslovakia for good. And that meant this was probably the last time I'd ever see any of them.

Leaving came at a great price for me. To some, Czechoslovakia means beautiful scenery, medieval castles, Pilsner beer, and cruises down the Elbe River. But to me, it means home, my childhood, and my youth, all of which I was leaving behind forever. Yet, I knew in my heart that I had to go.

My mother stood next to me until I reached the boarding gate and handed my ticket to the clerk. If there was ever a time to say "I love you," this was it, but we Czechs don't do that—ever. So, she wished me well, hugged and kissed me fiercely, and reluctantly let me go. Once I reached the tarmac where the plane was waiting, I took one last look at the terminal behind me and saw my mother, sister, and friend crying and waving to me. I waved back and, in floods of tears, hurried up the plane's stairs before I could change my mind. Or before the police appeared out of nowhere to haul me off to jail because they knew I was about to defect.

I'd known from the age of nine that I wouldn't be living in communist Czechoslovakia anymore once I grew up, although I can't explain how or why I was so sure of this. Maybe I'd picked up on my mother's dream—she had always wanted to leave the country permanently, although that wasn't even remotely possible for her. Or maybe it was because I was always enamored of the U.S. and all things Western. Whatever the reason, I was absolutely certain there was something different, something better, waiting for me out there.

Some thirteen hours after boarding the plane, I began to understand what that "something better" was. After staggering half-dazed off the plane at JFK Airport in New York, I suddenly realized that I was free. I could smell the freedom as it washed over me, and my heart was filled to bursting with hope. I knew it was the beginning of my new life.

My old life began on December 22, 1968, when I, Jana Kandlova, was born in Ústí nad Labem, a major industrial center located in northwest Czechoslovakia, about a 30-minute drive from the German border. Ústí nad Labem (popularly called "Ústí") is located in a mountainous area called North Bohemia, about 50 miles north of Prague, and sits at the confluence of the Elbe and Bilina rivers, making it the perfect site for a river port. The area around it is loaded with natural resources like timber, coal, clay, and land that is so rich in minerals it's perfect for growing crops. For these reasons, Ústí was (and is today) an important site for farming, mining, manufacturing, and shipping. By the mid-twentieth century, it had become one of the most heavily industrialized areas in all of Europe.

The history of Czechoslovakia stretches back at least 1,500 years. Legend has it that Forefather Čech led his people to settle in Bohemia, which means "country of God." It might have seemed heavenly, but this little area of the world was the site of endless fighting, with the Czechs alternately sharing and fighting over it with neighboring Slovaks, Germanic tribes, and others. They did manage to establish their own kingdom for a while, but over time, maintaining independence became impossible, and by the mid-18th century, Bohemia became part of the Austro-Hungarian Empire. Nearly two hundred years later, at the end of World War I, when the Empire fell, the Czechs were joined by their neighbors, the Slovaks, to form a new nation called Czechoslovakia.

The country maintained its independence for about twenty years. Then the Nazi war machine took over Austria and started pressuring Czechoslovakia to surrender large swaths of the western part of the country (known as the Sudetenland). Although Czechoslovakia asked England and France for support, it was left to sink or swim on its own.

In 1938, the Nazis took over the Sudetenland and quickly turned whatever was left of Czechoslovakia into a police state. They used propaganda to turn neighbor against neighbor, dividing and weakening the people. Then they started draining the country of goods and natural resources, which were used to prop up the German economy. Entire chemical and steel factories were picked up and moved from Czechoslovakia to Austria, where they were used to churn out goods for the German war machine.

Throughout Czechoslovakia, the Nazis set up forced labor camps and death factories, the most famous of which was Terezin, a combination ghetto-concentration camp located inside the walls of an old fortress called Theresienstadt. (I went to high school right next door to what remains of this place.) Tens of thousands of Jews were killed at Terezin, with more than 80,000 others deported to various extermination camps. The Czechoslovakians suffered horribly during the war. More than 300,000 were murdered—in the camps, fighting on behalf of Czechoslovakian freedom, or as victims of the police state.

When the war finally ended in 1945, Czechoslovakia was freed from Nazi rule, only to be is swallowed up by the Russians, who swarmed in and propped up the Communist Party of Czechoslovakia. By 1948, the communists were so powerful they controlled the entire country. They seized property from anybody who still owned it, and those who believed in freedom were either hanged or sent to jail. No one was allowed to own weapons, and anyone who complained about the government might be thrown out of a window. The religious were persecuted, and the clergy was tortured. And while many churches continued to stand, they were treated like museums—pretty to look at, but not functional.

Once the communists took over, just about the only thing left of Czechoslovakia's past was its name. In total control of jobs, housing, education, the media, and more, the communists systematically began to erase Czech history and culture. They insisted that the Czechs see themselves as proud communists, heirs to Lenin and Stalin, rather than to Forefather Čech. Communist history, philosophy, economics, education, and "scientific atheism" took over, and those who protested were arrested, dismissed from their jobs, ousted from their homes, or worse.

Slowly losing their identity, choking on pollution spewed out by newly-built factories, and lining up to buy the meager supplies available in stores, the Czechs and Slovaks struggled under communist rule. People were expected to call each other "comrade." They dutifully voted, even though there was only one party and one candidate, because refusing to vote could get them into trouble. Their children were taught to sing the Russian national anthem and salute the Russian flag. The Czechs lost not only their freedom and identity but also their souls.

Then, in January 1968, a “miracle” occurred—the Prague Spring. The reformist Alexander Dubcek, a new leader of the Czechoslovakian Communist Party, saw that heavy-handed communism was destroying the economy. He came up with a plan called “Socialism with a Human Face” that relaxed state control of the economy and allowed some freedom of speech. The people loved it and embraced it wholeheartedly. But a little taste of freedom always makes people hungry for more, and the Russians soon became afraid that Czechoslovakia was slipping out of their grasp. So in August, just eight months after the beginning of the Prague Spring, the Russians clamped down with a vengeance. More than half a million troops armed with the latest weapons invaded Czechoslovakia, many of them riding in Soviet tanks. Just like that, the Czechoslovakian’s little taste of freedom went out the window, sending them right back to where they started—a nation of dutiful, miserable, hopeless “comrades.”

My mother was pregnant with me during the Russian invasion, and when she heard the tanks rumbling up the street, she ran to the window of our apartment to see what was happening. Thinking there must be a parade going on, she waved gaily at the soldiers in their tanks as they rolled by. She knew nothing of the invasion because the news hadn’t yet reached Ústí, so she was surprised when the soldiers returned her waves with glares and shaking fists. When a couple of them suddenly pointed machine guns at her, she leaped away from the window in shock.

The Russian invasion was the beginning of a terrible new chapter in Czechoslovakian history. By the time I was born in December of that year, communism had regained its stranglehold on our country, and the Prague Spring was nothing but a distant memory.

I grew up in a southern suburb of Ústí nad Labem, just north of Střekov Castle, a 14th-century Gothic fortress perched high on a cliff overlooking the River Elbe. Across the river and a bit north of us, the ruins of a magnificent Art Nouveau mansion called Větruše sat on an equally high cliff. That cliff is a part of the mineral-rich Ore Mountains, which form a natural border between our country and Germany. With its beautiful scenery and amazing historic buildings, the area was once like the setting of a fairytale—until the Russians took over at the end of World War II. They completely transformed Ústí, making it into a major industrial center that cranked out massive amounts of engineering products, glass, ceramics, and textiles, among other things.

The beautiful Ore Mountains suddenly became major sites for the mining of lignite, also known as brown coal. Large areas were cleared of trees, plants, and topsoil, destroying wildlife habitats and triggering soil erosion, flooding, and water pollution. Ústí's historic center and most of its other old buildings were destroyed to make way for chemical plants that sprang up on the left bank of the river, producing dyes, sulfuric acid, varnish, and fertilizers. On the right bank, there were plants that manufactured soap, margarine, vegetable oil, and baking powder. Shipping and rail transport in the area were expanded, and almost overnight, our city became the most important river port on the Elbe.

The communists didn't care at all about the loss of our historic buildings, the stripping of our land's natural resources, or the massive increase in pollution caused by the new factories. They were only interested in manufacturing whatever products they needed and skimming off a huge share of the profits. Our beautiful city and its surroundings were sacrificed to satisfy their unending greed. The only reminders of old Ústí that were still left were the mighty Střekov Castle and Větruše, sitting untouched on their high cliffs, silent witnesses to the rape of the once-beautiful land below.

My family lived in a small two-bedroom apartment above the Elbe, just uphill from a soap factory that manufactured bath soap, bath bubbles, dish and laundry soap, and toothpaste, among other things. Like almost all factories in the area, it satisfied its gargantuan energy needs by burning the brown coal that was hauled in from local strip mines. Brown coal was prized by the communists because it was cheap and plentiful. But it was also one of the dirtiest fuels in the world, generating huge amounts of dust, carbon dioxide, sulfur dioxide, and nitrogen oxides. When these last two compounds were released into the air, they caused a chemical reaction that created acid rain. Inhaling them for just 24 hours could cause respiratory diseases like asthma. Although several factories in our area poured this stuff into the air almost constantly, no one in power seemed at all concerned. Not surprisingly, smog, haze, and smoke hung in our air no matter what the season, and asthma was extremely common.

Because we lived so close to the soap factory, not only was the air dirty, it also smelled horrible. The manufacturing of soap involves the cooking of things like bones and pine tar, which create a real stink. When these emissions were released, the air around us smelled like chemical farts. Another nearby factory sometimes released emissions that smelled like cigarette smoke. Because both factories released their emissions on a schedule, we didn't have to endure these smells every day. But when they let loose, it was very unpleasant, to say the least.

My father was a TV repairman who had a real gift for electronics and technology; he literally could put anything together. At age sixteen, he developed a burning interest in ham radios, and bought and assembled a radio kit all by himself. Before he was allowed to do this, however, he had to join an association of ham radio operators that was monitored by the Communist Party. This was the way so many things were done—you needed permission, a license, or membership in a particular association before you could do anything out of the ordinary.

Whatever effort it took for him to get into ham radios, however, turned out to be worth it. Ham radio operation has been a lifelong interest for him and given him countless hours of pleasure contacting people all over the world. It also came in handy during his two years of service in the Czechoslovakian military, when he became a radio operator at a missile launching station. He joined the Communist Party at that time, not because he wanted to, but because it was a prerequisite for his new job.

In 1968, during the Prague Spring, he found a different use for his ham radio equipment, taking it up into the hills to send details of the Russian invasion to the West. Because the communists had shut down Czechoslovakia's official radio station, the outside world didn't know what was happening. Dad went up into the hills to send messages about the Prague Spring and the Russian invasion several times, knowing full well that if the communists found out, he would be in big trouble. Some might say he was a hero of the resistance.

He *was* arrested for his actions—twice. Each time, he was interrogated for five straight days, all day and all night, but he refused to say a word. When the communists finally realized he wasn't going to reveal anything, they released him. But they also kicked him out of the Communist Party and labeled him "politically unreliable." Neither of these bothered Dad one bit.

In the 1980s, Dad's gift for technology served him well when he began learning about computers. By the mid-1980s, he began developing an integrated system for homes and hotels that controlled heating, electricity, hot water, lights, and whatever else a computer might regulate inside a building. Today, systems like these are quite common, but they were unheard of at the time. Dad also invented a turbine control system that was used in pools to teach indoor surfing. After the fall of the Soviet Union, he partnered with another man and formed a software company called Martia. When he sold his share of the company years later, he became a wealthy man. He was one of those lucky people who managed to find his way, in spite of living under communism for over 40 years.

My mother was a dental technician by trade who later became a teacher in that profession. Artistic, smart, and a hard worker, Mom could easily have become a clothing or jewelry designer if she hadn't been held down by communism. To have had an artistic career, she would have needed connections, plus government permission to earn more money than other people. Of course, she had neither of these, so her dream of being a designer vanished into thin air.

Mom had wanted to leave Czechoslovakia ever since the invasion of '68 when those Russian soldiers pointed machine guns at her, but my father was totally against it. I remember one time when our family secured permission to take a vacation to Italy. Then someone reported Dad to the government, saying he had been aware that a certain family had plans to defect but had not reported them. In response, the government barred Dad from going on vacation with us. Dad, in turn, refused to let the three of us go, so our vacation was canceled. Much later, my mother told me that Dad knew if she left the country with both of us kids, we'd all be gone forever. He was right.

I had a great relationship with my mother. She was my rock; the person I trusted most in the world and went to for everything I needed. Like most mothers, she took care of everything having to do with the house and the kids: the baking, cooking, cleaning, making of clothes, laundry, and so on. Another reason we were close is that we were fellow subordinates in Dad's kingdom. He had all the authority and control in our family and was tough to get along with, to say the least. All of us had to tiptoe around because he couldn't stand any noise, especially if he was on his ham radio. And there was no talking in the car—he found it distracting. If he didn't like what you were doing, he made sure you knew it.

Although my parents' relationship wasn't great, I can't remember ever hearing them fight. My guess is that Mom, who was very easy going, just let Dad have his way. We never talked about such things or anything else that you might call emotional. Still, we were close. Once, when I was ten years old, I was having trouble falling asleep, so she and I sat together and watched the movie "The African Queen" on television. I remember her explaining what the actors were saying and doing. It was one of those warm, cozy times that lives in my memory forever, just my mother and me enjoying each other's company. I felt safe with her, then and always.

Ever since I came to America, people have asked me what it was like to grow up in a communist country. I'm often surprised by how little they know about communism, other than it's evil and the people are treated horribly. So, before I continue with my story, I'll try to explain what communism is (or is supposed to be), and what it means to those who live in its clutches.

In the simplest terms, communism is a political and governmental system designed to create an idyllic world where all citizens are equal, with each person contributing according to his or her abilities and being rewarded according to his or her needs. All of the property is publicly owned, and the government provides the people with everything they need: food, clothing, housing, education, and so on. There are no social classes, which means no one can lord it over anyone else. There is no poverty; no lack of education; no "haves" or "have nots." Everyone is exactly the same, and all have equal opportunities to blossom, express their talents, and enjoy their lives. That's communism, at least in theory.

It sounds like it could be a good idea. Who wouldn't want to live in a society where everyone is equal and the government guarantees that your needs will always be provided for? But in reality, almost no one wants to live in such a society. The most obvious reason is there is no freedom for the average person. The ability to think for yourself, form and express your own opinions, and do what you want to do (without endangering others) is effectively outlawed. You can't own property, worship your own God, or take part in normal economic activity, like owning your own business. You can't speak your mind or write anything that the government doesn't approve of. You can't protest or own a weapon. My mother summed it up nicely when she said, "The communists tell you what to think, which words to use, what's good for you and what's bad." In short, people are treated like children who need every aspect of their lives tightly controlled at all times.

How do the communists control you? It's simple: since the government owns everything, it has the power to give and the power to take away. If you do what you're supposed to do, you'll get things. If you don't, you won't.

As a citizen, you are completely dependent upon the government to tell you where you can live, what you can eat, what work you must do, where you can go, and so on. There may be some people who don't mind this. Blindly following the rules can take away the burden of having to think or make decisions. I find that I feel this way when I go to my hot yoga classes. The teachers treat us like we're in boot camp and tell us exactly which exercises to do and how many of each. I'm okay with this because I know I probably wouldn't do the exercises if left on my own—and I love the classes and my teachers. But that's not communism. The difference between communism and hot yoga is I signed up for hot yoga, and I can choose to leave the class at any time. Under communism, *they* sign you up, and you can't leave, ever.

Another major reason that no one wants to live under communism is it just doesn't work. Throughout the 20th century, country after country succumbed to communist rule, then suffered from one economic, social, and environmental disaster after another. Think of Chernobyl, the killing fields in Cambodia, and the disastrous Cultural Revolution in China. Communism didn't work anywhere, not in Russia, China, North Korea, Vietnam, Venezuela, Poland, Hungary, East Germany, Somalia, Congo, Armenia, Ethiopia, or Czechoslovakia.

Whatever it was that the communists promised didn't come to pass. There was no equality; a tiny percentage of people held all the power and most of the wealth. Authoritarianism and corruption ran rife. Workers were paid low wages at their government-assigned jobs, so poverty increased to gargantuan proportions, and they lost their incentive to be productive or make quality goods. The old saying, "We pretend to work, and they pretend to pay us" held true. People who wanted to leave the country and go somewhere offering greater opportunity were forced to stay under threat of death. Borders were closed, and walls were erected. One hundred seventy years after the conception of communism, its biggest claims to fame are tyranny, oppression, and the murder of as many as 100 million people who refused to bend to its rules.

So how did this terrible form of government ever get a foothold? Its roots lie partially in human nature. From the beginning of time, the powerful have always lorded it over the powerless; in the ancient Roman Empire, throughout the Middle Ages, during the Renaissance, and later, royalty and the aristocracy routinely ran roughshod over the peasants. Slavery was common throughout Europe, Asia, the Middle East, Africa, and the Americas. Entire races or religions were marginalized and persecuted. Average people didn't have much to look forward to. Just getting through life, keeping the family intact, having a little fun, and praying for a better time in the afterlife was all they could hope for.

Then things started to improve. Slavery was outlawed in Europe and the Americas. A small middle class arose, made up of merchants, lawyers and doctors, and now and then somebody from a "low-born" family came to prominence. Still, a ruling class held almost all the wealth and power, while life continued to be difficult for the average person. This was especially true during the Industrial Revolution when many people left their farms and went to work in factories that paid them poorly and subjected them to dangerous conditions. At home, they lived in crowded, filthy city slums.

This dynamic—power and wealth for a few and failed promises for the rest—prompted two German intellectuals, Karl Marx and Friedrich Engels, to dream of a world that didn't have wealthy and poor, rulers and ruled, or owners and workers; where there was no struggle between the classes over power and money. In their book, *The Communist Manifesto,* and later Marx's *Das Kapital*, they spelled out their ideas for the creation of a utopian society. Private ownership of a business or factory would be replaced by communal ownership, so no one person would own anything. Instead, everyone would have a share of everything and work together for the good of the whole. Eventually, once this system got rolling, the government would fade away, replaced by groups (communes) that wisely and unselfishly made decisions that benefited the whole. Since everyone would have the opportunity to serve on a commune, everyone would have a voice in society.

In short, everyone would be equal to everyone else. All would enjoy freedom and have everything they needed to live happy lives. As a result, there would be no more wars.

The first to go for broke with this plan was Russia's Bolshevik party. In 1917, led by Vladimir Lenin, the Bolsheviks overthrew the Russian government and soon thereafter executed Tsar Nicholas II and his family. Lenin and his followers immediately began to crush all other political parties and organizations in Russia, arresting and murdering those who resisted. Ultimately, the Bolsheviks became the Communist Party of the Soviet Union.

Although the communist utopia described by Marx and Engels may sound like the world's greatest idea, the results were just the opposite. During the 74 years that the communists ruled Russia, millions of people lost their lives, some through mass arrests and phony trials, others through widespread starvation caused by the government seizing the land owned by farmers, then forcing them to work on collective farms that couldn't produce enough food to go around. The government's stranglehold on all decisions about production and investment caused the economy to wither. Most of the workers were poorly paid and were forced to live in small, run-down quarters. Shortages of just about everything were common.

Opposition and rebellion became huge problems, met head-on in the 1930s by communist leader Joseph Stalin, in what became known as Stalin's Great Purge. More than 750,000 people were killed when he eliminated dissenting members of the nation's Communist Party and anyone else he considered a threat. Over one million others were sent to gulags, the Soviet version of concentration camps.

What about those lofty ideas about everyone being equal and free, with all needs taken care of? As anyone who has lived under communism will tell you the individual is completely insignificant—unless he or she happens to be a VIP. The vast majority of people live under the watchful eye of the state police and civilian informers (often their own neighbors). Any dreams of a better life for themselves and their children are crushed. They must keep their heads down and their mouths shut, just to survive. And they can't leave.

My parents were used to communism, or so it seemed. They never talked about it. Maybe it was because they were born shortly after the war when the Russians first occupied our country, so communism and oppression were all they had ever known. Or maybe they felt there was no reason to complain since it wasn't going to change anything. They certainly didn't love it, but they didn't seem horribly upset about it, either.

But I hated it.

Chapter Two

Just Another Day in Commie Paradise

As far back as I can remember, the sound I dreaded most was the call of the mourning doves. Some people might find their sad, cooing sound to be soothing or even nice, like notes played on an old wooden flute. But to me it meant only one thing: it was time to get up and go; to leave our apartment and make my way out into a harsh, decayed, and depressing world.

I wasn't alone; my sister Eva, who is three and a half years younger than me, felt that way too. Eva was my constant companion, like it or not, unless I was actually in class at school. As her older sister, it was my job to take care of her. One of the first chores of my day was to take her to daycare in the morning, which was on my way to school. So, once we were dressed and had eaten our breakfast, off we'd go, plunging into the smog and smoke and inhaling the stinking emissions from the soap factory down the hill. With dead and dying trees all around us, we would trudge up the crumbling old road that led to the daycare center, where I'd drop Eva off, then go on alone to my school.

I never liked school. My mother says that when she walked me to my first-grade class on the first day of school, I took one look into that dark and dreary building and said firmly, "I'm not going in there." Mom pulled me inside anyway, but as she hung my coat in the closet, I grabbed a hook on the wall, held on to it, and wouldn't let go. The teacher came over and pulled me out of the closet with the hook still in my hand and hauled me into the classroom. It wasn't a promising beginning.

You'd think I would have been used to the idea of school by then because, like just about everybody else, I'd been institutionalized almost from the start. The communist ideal was to have both parents working at all times, so babies (including me) were typically enrolled in government-run childcare at about the time of their first birthday. This practice was so universal that during my childhood, I knew of only one woman who was staying home to raise her children. It all seemed very strange to me—even wrong. What was she doing at home? Why wasn't she out doing real work?

As it turned out, I was right to be wary of school. The teachers were very strict. If you acted up or made a mistake, they told you to go stand behind the door. If you gave the wrong answer, they sometimes made fun of you. They watched you carefully and could discipline you at any moment. It would begin with the teacher having a talk with you, followed by a note sent home to your parents who, in turn, would give you a beating. Everyone was afraid of being disciplined at school, not just because of the note sent home, but because no one wanted to be thought of as "a bad person." I had many notes sent home, mostly because I was either fighting with someone or talking to the person next to me.

The implanting of communist ideology into our brains started very early. We were always made to stand when the teacher walked into the room in the morning, and referred to him or her as "Comrade." Even in preschool, pictures of the Czechoslovakian and Russian presidents were tacked up on the wall. Whenever we sang the Czechoslovakian anthem in school, we also had to sing both the Russian anthem and the Internationale, a standard of the socialist movement. These last two songs were also played on the radio every single morning when I was very young, and all three anthems were sung at big hockey and soccer matches, or whenever anything else important happened.

The love of Russia and communism was constantly shoved down our throats. We heard a lot about the wonderful October Russian Revolution, celebrated every year with movies and parades on November 7. (Their calendar had been changed.) As we did on all public holidays, we had to wear red ties and red ribbons, and even the daycare centers held little tea parties for the kids. No one ever breathed a word about the massacre of the Russian royal family, on this day or any other. All we ever heard about the Tsar and his family was that they were bad, as were all royalty and capitalists. At age nine, we started learning the Russian language, and I can recall a big communist song competition being held at our school every year in the spring. We saw endless movies about World War II, in school and on television, all of which told the story of the "heroic Russians" who swooped in and saved us from the terrible Nazis. There was always a big celebration held on May 9, the day the Nazis surrendered to the Allies at the end of World War II.

In the first grade, we had to join a "scouting" group run by the Communist Party called "Little Star," that was a lot more about propaganda than learning to camp or tie knots. As we grew older, we progressed to becoming "Pioneers," then "Comrades" in the Young Communist League, which went on until we left school. At that point, we could decide for ourselves if we wanted to become members of the Communist Party. If so, we had to apply and prove ourselves worthy. Everybody knew by then that in order to get anywhere, you would have to belong to the party. Even if you just wanted a position like being a supervisor in a company, you would, at the very least, have to "get educated," which involved taking and passing a class in Marxism and Leninism. If you wanted to go to college, you would be studying these subjects in depth.

On May 1, International Workers Day (the communist equivalent of Labor Day in the U.S.), officials, children in the Pioneer movement, factory workers, and many others marched in a big parade. May 1 was a holiday in the sense that we didn't go to work or school, but definitely not a vacation day. No one, old or young, was allowed to stay home or do anything other than go to the parade; you could get in big trouble if you skipped it. This wasn't much of a problem, though, since everything was closed that day, and there was nowhere else to go. Even people like me, who weren't the least bit interested, went to the parade, if only for lack of better things to do.

School was never my thing; I found it utterly boring and uninspiring, never studied, and didn't care about what they tried to teach us. The only things I liked were art and music, but the fun was ruined because both were always aimed at teaching us to love communism or Mother Russia. At the age of five, I remember drawing a picture of the famous Russian navy cruiser "Aurora," celebrated for firing the first shot of the Russian Revolution. The teacher put a model of the ship on a table and told us to draw it. I did a pretty good job, but it would have been a lot more fun if we were drawing a house or a bunch of flowers. But the communists would have seen this as a waste of time. I'm happy to say that none of their brainwashing worked with me. Even as a little girl, I never liked the Russians. As far as I was concerned, they were all bad.

At the end of the school day, I'd walk back to the daycare center to pick up Eva. Then, I'd shepherd her to our after-school activities, if we had any, which sometimes involved riding on city busses. By the time I was eight years old, I was able to get around by bus with no problem. It's not that I was so mature for my age (although I can't imagine my ten-year-old daughters doing this today). Where I grew up, all of the kids had to learn to be responsible at a young age. Most of us started making trips to the grocery store by the time we were five, armed with a list and a bag.

Once my sister and I finally made it home from school, I'd babysit her until my parents got home from work. During this time, I'd do chores that included doing the dishes, dusting, taking out the trash, setting up for dinner, mopping the floors, and sometimes cleaning the staircase of the apartment building. In addition, I would supervise Eva while she did her chores. Naturally, she never wanted to do any of them, but if our parents got home and Eva's chores weren't done, *I* was the one who would get a beating. I tried to make her behave, mostly to protect myself, and we'd end up battling it out. Eva was never afraid, though, no matter how young she was. She's a true Czech; strong and unbreakable. You'd have to kill her before she'd give in.

The best parts of my young life were my visits to my grandparents, Babča and Děda, my mother's parents. They lived on a farm in a small town called Hrádek nad Nisou, where, to my delight, they had goats, pigs, chickens, and other animals. Since they lived only about an hour away by car, I went to their house a lot—and it became my heaven on earth.

It wasn't that the house itself was a big deal. Babča and Děda didn't even have indoor plumbing, just an outhouse that smelled horrible in the summertime. In the winter, it was a dark and scary place, especially if you had to go out there at night. Because it wasn't heated, your rear end would freeze to the toilet seat if the last person hadn't wiped it off. Děda finally brought a bucket into the house for these nighttime trips, which made things a lot easier.

It also wasn't that the area around the house was so wonderful. Everyone in Hrádek nad Nisou heated their homes with the same brown coal that was used to run the factories in our area. So I could always see and smell the suffocating brown smoke in the air during the winter, and I usually came home from my grandparent's house with a headache.

No, the great part about visiting my grandparents was Babča and Děda themselves. I lived with them for two whole summers while my parents were working and wanted to make it permanent because they treated me so well. Babča seemed willing to let me do anything I wanted. And Děda was always easy-going, mellow, and very kind. I loved helping him with the farm animals, and one of my special jobs was collecting eggs from the chickens. Looking back, I have to laugh at how unconcerned we were about dirt and germs. If one of the eggs was cracked and smeared with chicken poop, rather than throwing it away, we'd just suck out its contents. Nothing was wasted!

Today, I think it's a miracle that my grandparents were able to create such a relaxed and loving environment, after what they'd lived through during their younger years. Babča, born in 1923 in Poland, was just a teenager when her father, a member of the intelligentsia, was killed by the Russians in the Katyn Massacre of 1940. The Russians had found it a lot easier to manipulate the Poles if they were without their leaders, so anybody who had any brains or money or power was considered worthy of execution. Thus, they murdered about 22,000 Polish military officers and members of the intelligentsia during the Katyn Massacre, which lasted for two months in the spring of

1940. The Russians pretended the Germans did it and fooled people for many decades.

Not long after Babča lost her father, her mother, who was of German descent, married a Nazi officer/doctor whose job was to "attend" to pregnant women living in concentration camps. By this time, the Nazis had taken over the whole of Poland and carved it up like a big turkey, breaking off chunks to share with the Russians. And they were on a fast track to commandeering most of the rest of Europe. So, to Babča, her mother's decision to marry a dreaded Nazi made her seem like the worst kind of traitor.

Never one to hold back her feelings, Babča berated her mother constantly about this. I can imagine her saying, "Those Nazi bastards stole our country, and you *married* one?" Then one day, seventeen-year-old Babča went too far and blurted out something so disrespectful that her mother turned around and backhanded her. Babča flew across the room, landed face-first on a bucket, and split her face open. Soon afterward, her mother sent her to Czechoslovakia to stay with distant family members—indefinitely. That's where she met my grandfather, Děda.

Babča's tumultuous early life left her with strong, irrevocable feelings about certain groups of people, feelings she wasn't afraid to share. She hated the Nazis for taking over her country. She also detested the Russians (those "liars and thieves") for constantly trying to steal more and more territory from Poland. And she loathed the communists, who had murdered the Russian tsar and his family, whom she believed were our distant relations. A strong, opinionated woman who insisted on thinking for herself, Babča was the only person in my life who ever taught me how to stand up for myself.

My grandfather, Děda, worked as a machinist and foreman in a factory that manufactured automobile parts. He was athletic (a soccer player), good looking and, from what I'm told, quite the ladies' man when he was young. Born in the northern part of Czech not long after the Russian Revolution, Děda, like Babča, lost his father when he was young. Děda's father, a railroad worker, suffered serious brain damage in a terrible train accident and was sent to live permanently in an institution. His mother went on to marry again, and as soon as Děda was old enough, they sent him away to work. Fortunately, that's where he met Babča.

There's no doubt that Babča and Děda went through tough times, but my other set of grandparents, my father's parents, had it even worse. My paternal grandmother, whom I called Babi, was born in Ukraine, the daughter of an engineer who was beheaded by Stalin in 1942. Although Babi's father was part of the intelligentsia, he wasn't rebellious and didn't deserve to die. Stalin was just looking to kill Ukrainians, especially those who were intelligent, and Babi's father was hauled away. The government would one day admit his execution was a mistake, pardoning him after Stalin died in 1953, for whatever that was worth.

Babi, nineteen years old when her father was executed, was sent, along with her mother, to a work camp in Germany. They were held in the camp for three long years, until the end of the war. The one good thing that happened was she met my grandfather, Děda Kandl, the bastard son of an Austrian nobleman. Born in Vienna in 1912 when it was still part of the Austro-Hungarian Empire, my grandfather's job at the camp was finding and disposing of unexploded bombs, so it's a miracle he made it through the war. Fortunately, he did, and shortly after the camp was liberated in 1945, he and Babi married. Soon thereafter, they had my father.

The "utopia" that the early communists dreamed of creating could be summed up in one sentence: "We do everything together, we share everything together, and everyone will have plenty." One of their major goals was that no one would ever have to look at someone else's plate and get upset because the other person had more. This goal, of course, was never realized.

Anyone who has ever lived under communism will tell you that there are always those who have more and others who have less. In order to get more, you need to know the right people and have money. Greater privileges were given to those who had ties to important government officials or relatives in Russia, were the children of doctors, or had higher salaries. But if you were smart, you always considered your privileges "gifts" from the government, gifts that could easily be taken back. "The government considers it all their money," a friend of mine used to say, "They just let you keep some of it." And not necessarily forever. This set-up allowed the government to take total control of our lives. Governmental authorities told us what to do, when to do it, and how. They also spelled out exactly what we couldn't do, and someone was always watching us, ready to report any behavior deemed "unacceptable."

Sometimes their ideas of unacceptable behavior were completely ridiculous. When I was in 6th grade, for example, my mother, a good seamstress, made me some nice clothes (nothing fancy) for school, using clothing catalogs from Germany as a guide. Then one of my teachers noticed my nice clothes and decided I was dressing better than the other kids. And, of course, no one was supposed to have more than anyone else. The next thing we knew, my mother was called to the school and reprimanded. She was told to use better judgment and not to send me to school in those clothes again.

This, of course, was just a small (but annoying) example of governmental interference. There were much more serious forms of control that extended to every part of our lives. For example, we weren't allowed to decide for ourselves which house or apartment we wanted to live in. We had to apply for a place to live and wait for something to come up, a process that could take as long as five years. Once something finally surfaced, we weren't given any choice—we could either take it or get back on the list and wait some more. Naturally, people who were "in" with the government got to live in much better places than those who weren't. And some people were stuck living with relatives indefinitely.

If you wanted to have more than just a bare minimum of money and possessions, it was absolutely crucial that you find a way around the endless government regulations. Lucky for us, my father was pretty good at talking his way into whatever he wanted. When he needed permission to take on a second job, he made sure he mentioned his Russian relatives as much as possible—and that worked. When we were looking for a place to live, he used this same ploy to get us into a decent building that was almost brand-new at the time. I learned early that you could either work the system or live with next to nothing.

The government started controlling its children's future very early in life. By the age of six, we kids were strongly urged to decide what we wanted to do when we grew up. By the age of ten, the teachers were already shaping us for our future careers. I wanted to become a veterinarian, but my teacher quickly informed me that girls don't do that. I then switched to kindergarten teacher, which became my career goal when I was hardly able to tie my shoes.

Once we started on a career path, our futures were pretty much carved in stone. At the end of middle school (age 14), we had to apply to high school prep school, trade school, or high school, depending on our chosen careers. Those aiming for professions requiring college or university degrees applied to a high school prep school. Those who wanted jobs that required special knowledge, but no college degree, applied to trade school. No college was required for my goal, which was to be a kindergarten teacher, for that was considered a trade school job. This meant college was not on my to-do list.

The next step, for all of us, was to take an entrance examination at our school of choice, which we either passed or failed. It was a major turning point in our lives. If we didn't pass the test, or if spaces in our desired career were not available, we failed and had to find another line of work.

The idea behind sorting children into groups that determine how much education they will get is typical of the communists. They don't want to waste time and money teaching children anything they don't need to know. The problem is that most kids don't know enough about the world to choose what they want to do with their lives at age six or even ten. Still, we got locked in early, and found out later that it was next to impossible to make changes. Once we had been educated or trained to do a particular job, our chances of switching to something else were practically nonexistent.

Jobs and careers, like everything else, were parceled out by the government. If you were lucky enough to be offered a job, it was often paired with duties that were unappealing. Let's say you wanted to teach physical education. You might be offered a job in that field, but it also included teaching a couple of classes in advanced math. Never mind that you're not good in math and have no interest in the subject. You're doing it, or you can wait a long time to be offered something else. So many people ended up doing jobs they didn't like. Wages and incentives were low, and getting fired from a job was rare, so some people just showed up for work and did nothing. Thus the famous saying, "Under communism, they pretend to pay us, and we pretend to work."

It's not too surprising that this dreary, hyper-controlled environment turned most of us into dreamers. Our dreams, though, weren't about opening a neighborhood business, or creating the next Amazon.com, or making life better for those who came after us. Everybody's big dream, or so it seemed, was to have a "country house." By that, I don't mean a cute little chateau on a plot of land next to a lake, or a cozy cabin nestled way up in the mountains. I mean a plain little bungalow just outside of the city that's more of a storage house than a real place to live.

It might not sound very appealing, but anywhere we could go to escape the noise, smells, and oppression of the city seemed like heaven. In the city, we lived our lives under the government's thumb, constantly being told what to do. We were watched and reported if we did or said anything wrong. Those who were lucky would get off with just a warning. Those who weren't might end up in a gulag or disappear off the face of the earth. This constant pressure made us desperate to escape to the countryside on the weekends, where we could relax and enjoy a little bit of freedom. Those who couldn't afford a country house would go out into nature to hike.

With this in mind, my father, uncle, and paternal grandparents bought a little house just outside of town that was about the size of a two-car garage. There was no indoor plumbing; it had an outhouse down the hill that was closed in the winter, so the house only functioned during three seasons.

It wasn't set up for sleeping or sitting on a couch reading—we used it mostly for storage. But my mother and grandfather liked to go there to garden. My uncle often showed up with cigarettes, a six-pack, and a deck of cards, looking for a good card game. And I liked to go just to get out of the city. In those days, everyone lived for the weekends and counted the days until we could escape to our own little piece of paradise.

I knew I wasn't going to stay in Czechoslovakia forever. But certain events happened, one after another, that pushed me to decide to leave the country. The first occurred at the end of middle school when I didn't pass a crucial math test, and my dream of becoming a kindergarten teacher vanished into thin air. My parents scrambled around and were finally able to get me into a college prep high school, but it didn't feel good to find that my long-term goal was suddenly unreachable.

The second event was that I started listening to the radio programs "Voice of America" and "Free Europe." For the first time, I heard people who had escaped from communism talking about the difficulty of life under communism, and about Czechoslovakia's disposal of intellectuals and others who might be able to lead the people to a freer kind of life. They talked about not being able to leave the country because the government wouldn't allow it.

All of this was news to me. Believe it or not, for the longest time, I didn't even know that being unable to leave the country was wrong. Once someone pointed it out and I realized it wasn't right, I felt like I had a heavy weight pressing down on my head, always. I started playing the guitar and learning anti-government songs. My friends and I would gather in somebody's home or sit outside around a fire pit, playing and singing our songs. It was illegal; we could have gotten into trouble. But for some reason, we didn't.

None of the kids I knew talked about politics, but we often talked about the material things we wanted, practically all of which were Western: toys, sports equipment, and clothes, all nearly impossible to come by. Certain Western clothes, like t-shirts decorated with American flags or the logos of Western rock bands, were out-and-out banned. Naturally, this just made them more appealing.

My sister and I got into collecting anything we could find that was Western: empty tennis ball cans, chewing gum wrappers, even empty Coke cans. All of these had once held products that weren't available to us, making them seem valuable. We displayed our "treasures" to other kids as status symbols, a sort of "I have it, and you don't" kind of thing. It was all just stuff that belonged in the trash can, but back then, these things represented the U.S. to me, which was sounding better and better all the time. Even when the nuclear reactor at Chernobyl exploded in 1986, and everyone said we'd been bombed by the evil Americans, the U.S. sounded like someplace I'd really love to go.

When I finished school, I got a job as a "governess" for a group of high school aged students doing internships to become salespeople at various stores. My aunt, who had a good relationship with the headmaster of the school, found the job for me. My duties were to make sure these kids, who were almost my age, arrived on time every day and did whatever they were supposed to do. I would accompany them to the store every day, and watch them learn things like how to wrap a bottle of wine for a customer or make change at a cash register. It was a ridiculous job that I really didn't like. But it was all I had going at the time, so I tried to throw myself into it. One of the things I did was volunteer to collect money from the kids for an upcoming after-school ski trip.

It was around this time that I decided to buy myself some Western clothes. Such clothes were still scarce but becoming more available to those who knew where to look. I knew a woman who had access to Western things, and wanted to get some jeans, a sweater, and some boots. So I cashed my paycheck and hurried off to make the purchase.

I was thrilled with my new clothes. But I had barely worn them out in public when someone reported me to the authorities at the high school. Whoever it was hinted (or said straight out) that I had stolen money from the student's ski trip fund to buy Western clothes because there was no way I could have afforded them otherwise. Just like that, I was under investigation. The school authorities came to my office, accused me of stealing student money, and refused to believe I'd paid for the clothes myself.

Without a word, I went to my desk drawer, took out the student money, and handed it to them; not a penny was missing. With nothing more to say, they turned and left my office. But I'd had it with the jealousy, spying, unfounded accusations, and hyper-controlling atmosphere. It was time to get out—out of my job and out of the country.

The seeds of my escape had been sown six years earlier in the summer of 1982, when I was 13. I was diving into a pond near Babča's house when I met a 14-year-old boy named David, and we started talking. When it was time for me to leave, he gave me a ride back to Babča's on his bicycle, even though it meant tossing his clothes into a dumpster because there wasn't room for them on the bike. It might sound silly now, but at 13, I found it incredibly cavalier. In my mind, he had swooped the clothes off the bike and casually thrown them aside, all for me—like in the movies. David and I exchanged addresses and soon became pen pals. I saw him only one more time when I happened to be boarding a train in my grandmother's town—he didn't know I'd been visiting—and he ran over to say hi. But we stayed pen pals for years. Even though we didn't see each other, he was my trusted friend, like a diary with a person on the other end. He was a great listener, and he always made me laugh.

David had an interesting and tragic background. In 1969, when he was 2 years old, his parents took a vacation to Switzerland, leaving him with his grandparents. While there, his parents decided they weren't coming back and tried to make arrangements for David to join them. The Czechoslovakian government, however, refused to approve his papers—there was too great a chance that the family would defect. His parents continued their stay in Switzerland and tried to find a way to be reunited with their son.

They finally decided to hire a professional smuggler, who would sneak David across the border along with a few other children. It was an incredibly dangerous plan, and, in the process, they were caught. The smuggler was shot and killed right before the children's eyes. David was returned to his grandparents in Czechoslovakia, and his parents were told that he would be sent to an orphanage because the grandparents were too old to raise him.

David's parents struggled for four years to get David out of Czechoslovakia, but eventually realized they had no choice but to return to Czechoslovakia and face the music. Once they arrived, they were kicked out of their apartment, they lost their jobs, their identification documents were confiscated, and they weren't allowed to travel anywhere outside of the local vicinity for years. Unable to work or make money and without a place to live, they moved in with David's grandparents. They ended up divorcing over this.

Amazingly, over a dozen years later, when David was 18, his family tried it again, this time going from Czechoslovakia to Italy, then attempting to immigrate to Australia (but being refused), and finally going to the U.S., where they settled in Hartford, Connecticut. All this time, David and I continued our pen pal relationship, although I had still only seen him twice.

At the end of 1987, David invited me to visit him in Connecticut. By then, he'd been living in the U.S. for three years and was fairly well established; he had a green card and was working as a carpenter. I was so fed up with my restricted life in Czechoslovakia and so enamored of the U.S. that it sounded like the opportunity of a lifetime. While neither of us put it into words, the idea was I would live with David, marry him, get a green card, and stay in the U.S. for good.

Getting my visas in order turned out to be surprisingly easy. I guess the officials thought a young girl like me, traveling alone, was sure to come back. Whatever the reason, I was able to secure a round-trip ticket to New York (under the pretense that I would be coming back). I was scared to death to make this huge, irreversible move, and told just about everyone I knew that I was going, hoping someone would stop me. The one person I didn't tell was my father, who definitely would have put a stop to it but never got the chance because he was on a business trip when I left. My new, free, independent life was suddenly within my grasp.

Chapter Three

Free at Last?

When I first arrived in the U.S., I was absolutely blown away by the idea that I was living in a country based on democracy and capitalism, which meant one thing to me: freedom. After spending my entire life being squelched by communism, I was finally free to live my life as I saw fit, with a minimum of governmental interference. Suddenly, I could speak my mind, go after whatever job or career I chose, and buy whatever I could afford without anyone breathing down my neck or insisting I follow endless rules. It was really hard to believe.

I remember driving and walking around my new city, Hartford, looking at the people on the street, the shops and restaurants, the parks and city squares, and thinking things like: "Wow, I can actually say anything I want here without getting arrested;" "I can buy a gun and keep it in my house if I feel like it;" "I can join a protest group, march around a park, and ask people to sign petitions;" or "I can buy and wear any kind of clothes I want without getting into trouble." Today, of course, I take these things for granted, but back then, it seemed like the ropes that had bound me all my life had suddenly been loosened.

The downside of my newly-found freedom was I would never again be able to return to Czechoslovakia. When a person defects, the government tries her in absentia, finds her guilty and administers punishment. I was found guilty of stealing from the Czechoslovakian government, stealing the money they had invested in my education and health care. Since they couldn't punish me directly, they did it indirectly. My sister, who was training to become a neonatal nurse, was no longer allowed to pursue her dream. It was a typical communist method of keeping people in line—if they couldn't punish the offender directly, they hurt her loved ones instead. That would teach others not to defect, out of fear that their families would suffer.

Fortunately, in 1989, just a year after I left, the communists lost their iron grip on the Eastern Bloc. When the Berlin Wall fell, everyone who believed in freedom rejoiced. It was wonderful for my parents in so many ways, not the least of which was they escaped being punished for "letting" me leave the country.

I could have returned to Czechoslovakia then without paying a price, but I never even considered it. I had too many unhappy memories of living under communist rule, and I was too enamored of freedom to be willing to give it up. In fact, for the longest time, I had nightmares in which my dad or someone else came to the U.S., found me, and tried to drag me back to Czechoslovakia. No way would I ever let that happen.

After living in the U.S. for over thirty years, I can honestly say I've never regretted my decision to uproot my old life and create a new one based on freedom. And yet I sometimes wonder just how free we really are. And I wonder how many of us are aware that the United States is sliding steadily toward socialism, which is so close to communism that I use the two terms interchangeably. For simplicity's sake, I'll refer to both as "socialism."

I don't mean to imply that the U.S. is on the brink of becoming a socialist country. There seems no danger that the country is about to be taken over by the Socialist Party USA or Communist Party USA. (Yes, they *do* exist, and they even have websites!) The chance of either of these parties gaining power in Congress and staging a *coup d'état*, the way they did in Czechoslovakia, is non-existent. The real danger is we Americans are slowly forgetting what it means to be free—and we seem to be unaware that socialism, which seems like such a nice, easy way to live, is a huge threat to our individual rights.

Socialism has a long history in the United States. Although it's hard to pinpoint exactly when socialist ideas began to take hold, certainly by the time the Great Depression hit in the 1930s, the government began acting in a socialistic manner.

Following the horrendous stock market crash in October 1929, the U.S. banking system floundered, factories closed, massive numbers of people lost their jobs, and the economy ground to a halt. People turned to the government for help, and beginning in 1933, the newly-inaugurated President Franklin Roosevelt implemented the "New Deal," a federal program that offered the people relief, reform, and recovery. Programs like the Civilian Conservation Corps hired people to build roads and work on forest conservation projects. The Farm Security Administration provided support to farmers, and the new Social Security system doled out money to retired people. Then the federal government tried to "fix" its broken financial system by passing laws designed to regulate the banks and shore up the economy.

Some of the New Deal programs were wonderful because they really did help people in need. Others were more like well-intentioned efforts to rev up the economy, some of which worked and some of which didn't. Right from the start, however, the entire program was controversial. People wondered whether the government should be allowed to grab so much control of the economy and the nation. When the Supreme Court ruled that several New Deal programs were unconstitutional, President Roosevelt hit back with a plan to "pack the court." He wanted to increase the number of Supreme Court justices from nine to fifteen and appoint six new ones who agreed with him, giving him a majority of votes on the court. Fortunately, his plan was quickly shot down in Congress.

Volumes have been written on the New Deal, but a key point is that the government's gargantuan efforts *didn't* solve the underlying problems. The Great Depression dragged on for more than ten years, until December 1941, when Japan bombed Pearl Harbor and the U.S. entered into World War II. With millions of men and women suddenly part of either the Armed Forces or the industries supporting them, the economy finally revved up and went into high gear.

The Ideal Government

The New Deal helped to put food in people's mouths and give them hope, but it was *not* the solution to the Great Depression. In fact, it proved that our problems can't be solved by a government making itself bigger and more powerful so it can give us food and jobs, create a lot of agencies, and pass endless laws. More government isn't ideal government. But what is ideal government? Thomas Jefferson defined it in his 1801 Inaugural Address, when he said it "shall restrain men from injuring one another, shall leave them otherwise free to regulate their own pursuits of industry and improvement, & shall not take from the mouth of labor the bread it has earned."[1]

In other words, the ideal government allows us to regulate our own lives while protecting us from harm, as in:

- Harm from outside enemies, meaning other countries or people who make war on us or harm us in indirect ways

[1] James McPherson, editor. **To The Best of My Ability**. New York, Dorling Kindersley, 2001. P317.

(for example, by preventing us from trading freely with other countries or by interfering with our elections);

- Harm from internal strife, by setting up police forces and criminal courts to arrest and punish dangerous people, and civil courts to help us settle our disputes;
- Harm from imperfect products, by setting standards and enforcing regulations that ensure that buildings don't fall down and poisons don't infiltrate our food supply.

Today we realize that another important job of the government is to build and maintain our infrastructure—our roads, airports, Internet, and other things that help us move around and communicate with each other. A good infrastructure binds the nation together by making it easier for people to travel, meet with others, exchange ideas, and conduct business across vast distances. It also helps us see ourselves as part of a nation, rather than as inhabitants of just a city or state, and this strengthens our country as a whole.

The ideal government, then, ensures freedom, maintains safety, and provides an infrastructure that binds the nation together. All of these should be accomplished efficiently, effectively, and with as light a hand as possible. At the same time, the government should stay out of people's personal business and refrain from taking money out of their pockets. And it should not force anyone to adopt anyone else's beliefs. That's it, in a nutshell.

Slipping from Ideal

As far back as when I was a teenager, I'd always seen the United States as a shining star of freedom. Maybe that's why it was so surprising and troubling when, a few years after I arrived, I started noticing indications that we Americans aren't really as free as I'd thought. Just to name a few, the government is amazingly bloated and intrusive. For example, it can determine exactly what children are to be taught in school, who can and cannot work numerous jobs, via licensing requirements, whether or not health insurance has to cover birth control, and more. These are all government restrictions on our freedom.

I also learned that there are certain things that you really aren't allowed to say (although they aren't actually illegal). You may be kicked out of college or lose your job over an innocent remark, or for bravely speaking your mind. This is a restriction on our freedom.

I discovered that certain groups are favored over other groups in several ways, including in the granting of government contracts, and for entry into universities. This is a restriction on our freedom.

These three things, and more, remind me of my life in communist Czechoslovakia. This erosion of our freedom is happening so slowly that most people aren't even aware of it, and probably won't be aware of it until things start to get bad. But socialism is insidious, and once it takes hold, it can be very difficult to weed it out. America is suffering from the slow and steady wearing away of our rights and freedoms, better known as "creeping socialism." And it breaks my heart.

If You'd Been There, You'd Know

Creeping socialism happens gradually and in such seemingly inconsequential ways that it seems trivial to most people. For example, some state governments have made it illegal for restaurants to give plastic straws to customers who order drinks unless they ask for them. People in Chicago are forced to pay a hefty 10.25% sales tax. I can't cut down dead trees in my back yard without a city permit. The *New York Times* has launched a major program called the "1619 Project" to reinterpret American history by placing slavery at its center.

Any one of these sorts of things by itself may be tolerable, and some may actually be helpful. That's not the point. The point is that we've become numb to the signs of creeping socialism.

We barely notice that government has crept into too many aspects of our lives to list, and that it has seduced and weakened us with promises of "free" this and that.

We quietly acquiesce when told to shut our mouths by the purveyors of political correctness, and we don't scream in protest when people's lives are ruined by runaway PC.

We stand idly by while our children are taught that our nation is evil, that white people and white men in particular are scourges.

We have yielded to the call to endlessly demand our liberties, yet ignore our responsibilities to ourselves, other people, and the nation as a whole.

All of these things, and more, subtract from our freedom. All of these things are happening now, but many of us don't see it. Or we do see it, but don't understand how dangerous it is. I see it, and I understand, because I've been there. I've seen what happens when the government is too large and intrusive, too powerful, and too determined to mold people. I've seen how the government seizes more power under the guise of protecting the environment, or something similar. I've seen what happens when you're not allowed to think certain thoughts or say certain things, when your history is rewritten, and you are taught to genuflect to the "right" ideas and people.

That's why I wrote this book, to help people recognize the signs and understand what is happening. To take the steps necessary to protect their freedom and to ensure that this country remains the shining star of liberty and prosperity, the country that people are willing to risk everything to get to.

In the chapters that follow, I'll take a look at the many ways in which we are creeping toward socialism—unknowingly or otherwise. These chapters are meant to be stand-alones, which means you can read them consecutively, or in any order you choose. Let's begin with government, which is growing to alarming proportions in size, reach, and ability to direct our everyday lives—even while much of it is way past its expiration date.

Chapter Four

Government by Goner

The highways of American history are littered with companies that have failed; even well known, sector-dominating companies have disappeared. You might remember some of their names: Blockbuster, Borders, F.W. Woolworth, Pan Am, General Cinema, Compaq, and Bear Stearns. All of them are "goners." They might be goners because they were inefficient, corrupt, unable to keep up with technological changes, or couldn't connect with their customers. Or maybe they were swept aside by larger economic or social forces. Whatever the reasons, once they no longer pleased their customers, they were gone. And that's a good thing.

The "disappearing company" phenomenon isn't at all unusual. While some companies last for decades, most don't. In one study, researchers looked at publicly-traded companies as far back as 1950[2] to see how long they survived before merging or being acquired by another company, going bankrupt or simply vanishing. The results were surprising: the average lifespan of a publicly-traded company is just ten years. And even those on the celebrated S&P 500 list typically only last twenty years,[3] no matter what kind of business they're in. That's how it should be. Once a company has outlived its usefulness or

---

[2] "This Is How Long Your Business Will Last, According to Science." By Rishi Iyengar. *Times*, April 2, 2015. Viewed February 10, 2020. Accessible at https://time.com/3768559/company-mortality-rate-survival-study/.

[3] "Why Half of the S&P 500 Companies Will Be Replaced in the Next Decade." By Ilan Mochari. Inc., March 23, 2016. Viewed February 10, 2020. Accessible at https://www.inc.com/ilan-mochari/innosight-sp-500-new-companies.html.

no longer performs well, it should be swallowed up by another firm or just swept off the table.

But does this same principle apply to our government? It should. Our government is made up of "companies" in the form of agencies, bureaus, committees, departments, etcetera. Yet how often are these various "companies" swept away because they're inefficient, corrupt, unsuccessful at connecting with their customers, or no longer useful? How often does our government do away with the goners? Not often enough. And that's a bad thing.

Smelling like Rotten Milk?

Let's look at the biggest "companies" in the federal government, the fifteen major departments headed by members of the President's Cabinet.

The State Department, Treasury Department, and Defense Department (formerly known as the War Department) were all part of our country's very first cabinet under President George Washington. Over time, other departments were added, including the Interior Department in 1849, the Agriculture Department in 1864, the Justice Department in 1870, and the Transportation Department in 1966. The Energy Department was created in 1977, which makes it forty-three years old as of this writing. The Department of Homeland Security was established in 2003, making it seventeen years old. Thus, even the baby of the bunch is well past the ten-year average lifespan of publically-traded companies, and close to the twenty-year life of most S&P 500 firms.

Many of these government "companies" are well past their expiration dates. Yet they go on and on, issuing endless regulations, distributing loads of money, and commissioning surveys and studies that do much to determine how the government, businesses, and people view the world and conduct themselves.

Most of these government "companies" suffer from serious cases of inefficiency, corruption, failure to connect with their customers, and inability to deal with the larger forces sweeping the nation and the world. Many of them have no justification for existing, other than they are there. So we, to a large extent, are being governed by goners.

Our Government Lacks "Creative Destruction"

Capitalism thrives on what's known as creative destruction, in which the old gives way to the new as innovations appear. Examples of creative destruction include Amazon replacing most book stores and a large number of other kinds of retail stores, music streaming practically wiping out CDs, and digital cameras in cell phones replacing hand-held cameras with old-fashioned film. And 3D printing is currently threatening to upend traditional manufacturing processes.

But our government takes a totally different approach. Because it doesn't have to compete in the marketplace, old government "companies" can be kept alive forever. Rather than replacing old attitudes, techniques, organizational structures, and so on, these things stay the same, while new "subsidiaries" and "branches" are layered on top of them in the form of departmental agencies, bureaus, centers, councils, offices, and the like. So we often have overlaps in authority, duplication of labor, the creation of fiefdoms, and other problems.

Take, for example, the confusing federal governmental overlap concerning food safety. The FDA (Food and Drug Administration) and the USDA (U.S. Department of

Agriculture's Food Safety and Inspection Service) shoulder most of the responsibility for inspecting food to ensure that it is safe. You would think there would be a clear, obvious, and logical division of duties—but that's not the case. For example, the USDA is in charge of dehydrated, frozen, and liquid eggs, while the FDA checks out eggs still in the shell. To make matters even more confusing:

> *The FDA inspects all fish except catfish, which are under the USDA's purview. Closed-faced sandwiches and bagel dogs are in the USDA's bailiwick, while open-faced sandwiches and corndogs are left to the FDA.*[4]

Making the situation even more confusing, the FDA oversees "[p]roducts with 3% or less raw meat" while the USDA handles those with more than 3%; the FDA oversees products with "less than 30% fat, tallow or meat extract, alone or in combination," while the USDA handles those with more than 30%; the FDA oversees "[c]heese pizza, onion and mushroom pizza," while the USDA handles pepperoni pizza and "meat-lovers stuffed crust pizza…"; the FDA oversees "rabbit stew, shrimp-flavored instant noodles, venison jerky, buffalo burgers, alligator nuggets, noodle soup chicken flavor" while the USDA handles "spaghetti sauce with meat balls, open-faced roast beef sandwiches, hot dogs, corn dogs, beef/vegetable pot pie."[5]

---

[4] "Bloated Federal Agencies Have Become the Norm. Here's the Key to Sizing Them Down." By John W. York. The Heritage Foundation, November 21, 2017. Viewed February 11, 2020. Accessible at https://www.heritage.org/government-regulation/commentary/bloated-federal-agencies-have-become-the-norm-heres-the-key-sizing.

[5] Information in this paragraph take from the U.S. Food & Drug Administration Investigations Operations Manual 2020. Exhibit 3-1, FDA/USDA Jurisdiction. Page 3-24. Viewed April 9, 2020. Accessible at https://www.fda.gov/media/113432/download.

Not only do these "companies" overlap their functions, but they're also often caught up in embarrassing lapses such as this one in 2014:

> *The State Department's inspector general has warned the department that $6 billion in contracting money over the past six years cannot be properly accounted for...*[6]

The inspector general also noted that the department's internal systems for keeping track of funds like these are deficient. No one's saying the money is gone forever, that it has been embezzled or might be sitting, forgotten in someone's desk drawer. But it's not being used the way it should be. And we're talking about six billion dollars, an amount that could buy 26,455 American families a new home,[7] cover the salaries of 100,000 teachers for a year[8] or pay the average cost of 155,038 weddings plus honeymoons.[9] So, where is it? Might this six

---

[6] "State Department inspector general issues alert over $6 billion in contracting money." By Karen DeYoung. *The Washington Post*, April. 3, 2014. Viewed February 11, 2020. Accessible at https://www.washingtonpost.com/world/national-security/state-department-inspector-general-issues-alert-over-6-billion-in-contracting-money/2014/04/03/8ebf465c-bb73-11e3-9a05-c739f29ccb08_story.html.

[7] "The most expensive and affordable states to buy a house, ranked." By Hillary Hoffower and Libertina Brandt. *Business Insider*, July 5, 2019. Viewed February 11, 2020. Accessible at https://www.businessinsider.com/cost-to-buy-a-house-in-every-state-ranked-2018-8.

[8] The average teacher salary is $60,000 per year. See "The Evolution Of U.S. Teacher Salaries In The 21st Century." By Niall McCarthy. *Forbes*, April 2, 2019. Viewed February 11, 2020. Accessible at https://www.forbes.com/sites/niallmccarthy/2019/04/02/the-evolution-of-u-s-teacher-salaries-in-the-21st-century-infographic/#58f6e3ce77f0.

[9] The cost of the typical wedding, including engagement ring, ceremony, reception, and honeymoon, is $38,700. See "More couples are taking on debt to have Instagram-worthy weddings. Here's how much it costs to get married in the US." By Hillary Hoffower. *Business* Insider, July 26, 2019.

billion dollars have been diverted from where it belonged and sent elsewhere? Whatever happened to it, it's *our* money, folks!

You might remember what happened when the federal government launched the Affordable Care Act, popularly known as Obamacare, back in 2013. The introduction of the new health insurance system and the HealthCare.gov website turned out to be a disaster, and even President Obama was forced to acknowledge that:

> *...the procurement systems, the specifications, the way that software was built in government was adapted for the age when procurement was for buying boots or buying pencils or buying furniture as opposed to buying software.*[10]

In other words, the government is often inefficient, ineffective, and stuck in the past, yet trying to run a huge and complex nation.

Time for the Broom?

Naturally, the comparison between capitalism and government has its limits. We don't, for example, want six departments of defense competing to sell the nation military services. A great deal of what the government does is dependent on continuity, so unrestrained creative destruction would be harmful.

Viewed February 11, 2020. Accessible at https://www.businessinsider.com/how-much-does-it-cost-to-get-married-average-wedding-2019-7.

[10] "Obama Looks to outsiders to Fix 'Big and Bloated' Government." By Tom Shoop. *Government Executive*, March 12, 2016. Viewed February 11, 2020. Accessible at https://www.govexec.com/management/2016/03/obama-looks-outsiders-fix-big-and-bloated-government/126621/.

But we really need to take a broom to certain sections of our government and clean them out, like storerooms that have become so overstuffed we don't even know what's in them anymore. Just take a look at the way the responsibility for food safety is spread out over five federal entities:

- The Food and Drug Administration, which "regulates all foods and food ingredients introduced into or offered for sale in interstate commerce, except for meat, poultry, certain processed egg products, and catfish…"[11]
- The U.S. Department of Agriculture, which is responsible for eggs not in the shell, meat and poultry, grading raw fruits and vegetables, and certifying organic production.
- The National Oceanic and Atmospheric Administration, which is responsible for certifying fish and shellfish.
- The Environmental Protection Agency, which is responsible for drinking water.
- The U.S. Department of Treasury's Alcohol and Tobacco Tax and Trade Bureau, which is responsible for inspecting breweries, distilleries, and wineries.

The responsibility for food-related issues is further spread out among various committees in the Senate and House of Representatives, including those handling Agriculture, Forestry, Nutrition, Health, Energy & Commerce, and Science, Space, and Technology. Not to mention the federal entities that oversee the way food is grown, shipped, stored, and sold, or that monitor the way food is purchased from other countries and imported.

---

[11] "Producing a Food Product that is Regulated by the FDA." U.S. Food & Drug Administration, content current as of May 7, 2019. Viewed April 9, 2020. Accessible at https://www.fda.gov/food/food-industry/producing-food-product-regulated-fda.

Suffice it to say, we have way too many agencies and committees involved in ensuring that our food supply is safe. It's a classic case of too much government. Why not just fold all of the food-related activities into a single entity, perhaps a Department of Growing, Selling, and Consuming Food? Simpler is always better.

We Need a Lean, Mean, Governing Machine

Creative destruction could and probably should be applied to the entire federal government, sweeping away whatever no longer works well, is horribly inefficient, or has outlived its usefulness. Unfortunately, it's unlikely to happen for several reasons, including:

- We have no idea how big the government actually is. See chapter 5 for more on this.
- We have no way to measure how effective the government is, and how to judge what should stay and what should go.
- Too many people get government goodies. Quite understandably, many people want to keep what they're currently getting, even if wide-ranging reform may benefit them in the long-run. Read about gobbling the government goodies in chapter 6.
- It's much easier for politicians to "fix" problems by adding a new agency or office, or whatever, than it is to dig deep, discover the underlying problem(s), and make the painful adjustments.

But the most important reason we probably won't apply creative destruction to our government is that we have the wrong expectations about it. When problems arise, most of us think about laws we need to pass, bureaucrats we need to employ, and money we need to spend. What we should be doing is asking ourselves how to trim the government down and function with *less* regulation, *fewer* bureaucrats, and *smaller* budgets.

Simply reducing the size of the government will do much to get rid of the overlapping of responsibilities, duplication of effort, and building of fiefdoms. A smaller government will need less money to function, and thereby have less money to lose. It will become less complex, making it more understandable, both to us and to our elected officials. And having fewer bureaucrats covering their you-know-what's will make it easier to identify the responsible party when something goes wrong.

Making the government smaller and leaner makes it more flexible, better able to respond to problems and changing demands, and better able to serve us and our country.

Chapter Five

How Much Government is There?

Just how much government is there in the United States on the federal, state, and local levels? This is important to know because if we don't, we can't tell if the government is too big, too small, or just right. Neither can we tell if it's protecting us from harm without robbing us of liberty or taking excessive amounts of money from our pockets, along with our individual rights.

To be honest, I don't know how much government there is. Do you? Do you know how many government entities wield power at the federal, state, county, and city levels—along with special districts for schools, fire control, libraries, and so on? Do you know how many laws, rules, and regulations have been written, and how much in the way of taxes, fees, and assessments you're currently paying?

We're all aware of the "obvious" government: the president and congress, the state governors and legislators, and the local mayors, councilmembers, and supervisors. But how about the less obvious government, all those federal, state and local agencies, all the bureaus, departments, and so on? They produce a huge portion of the rules and regulations we must follow, and they can take plenty of money out of our pockets in the form of fees, fines, and assessments, plus the cost of complying with their dictates. (That cost is nothing to sneeze at, for it may total $4 trillion per year, which works out to $13,000 for every woman, man, and child in the nation.)[12]

[12] "Government Regulation: The Good, The Bad, & The Ugly." Contributed to by Jerry Brito, J. Kennedy Davis, Jr., Christopher DeMuth, et al. Regulatory

So, how much "less obvious" government is there? How many rules and regulations have they passed? How many programs have they mandated? How many people work for them? How much of our money is being spent on all of this? And how much freedom have they taken from us?

Let's make it simpler by asking how much "less obvious government" there is on just the federal level. You might think you could find the answer with a quick Google search, or maybe a phone call to your congressperson. In truth, it's practically impossible to get a definitive answer. I did find an "A-Z Index of U.S. Government Departments and Agencies" offered by USA.gov,[13] which lists hundreds of federal bodies that influence our lives and spend our money.

There are departments of Agriculture, Commerce, Defense, Education, Energy, Health and Human Services, Homeland Security, Housing and Urban Development, Justice, State, Interior, Treasury, Transportation, and Veterans Affairs.

There are administrations including the Bonneville Power Administration, Economic Development Administration, Employment and Training Administration, Farm Credit Administration, General Services Administration, Occupational Safety and Health Administration, Research and Innovative Technology Administration, Veterans Benefits Administration, and Western Area Power Administration.

There are agencies such as Global Media, International Development, Toxic Substances and Diseases Registry, and more.

There are bureaus of Consular Affairs, Economic Analysis, Engraving and Printing, Indian Affairs, Industry and Security,

---

Transparence Project. Viewed January 21, 2020. Accessible at https://regproject.org/paper/government-regulation-the-good-the-bad-the-ugly/.

[13] "A-Z Index of U.S. Government Departments and Agencies." USAGov, undated. Viewed March 17, 2020. Accessible at https://www.usa.gov/federal-agencies/. USA.gov is part of the U.S. General Services Administration.

International Labor Affairs, Justice Statistics, Ocean Energy Management, Prisons, Reclamation, the Census, Fiscal Service, Transportation Statistics, and more.

There are centers of Food Safety and Applied Nutrition, Nutrition Policy and Promotion, Parent Information and Resources, Disease Control and Prevention, and Medicare and Medicaid Services, as well as the Woodrow Wilson International Center for Scholars.

There are councils which include Chief Acquisition Officers, Chief Financial Officers, Chief Human Capital Officers, Chief Information Officers, Economic Advisors, Environmental Quality, plus Integrity and Efficiency. And don't forget the President's Council on Fitness, Sports and Nutrition.

There are commissions on Fine Art, Civil Rights, International Religion Freedom, Presidential Scholars, the Delaware River Basin, Japan-United States Friendship, and Security and Cooperation in Europe—plus the Susquehanna River Basin Commission.

There are foundations such as the James Madison Memorial Fellowship Foundation, and the Morris K. Udall and Stewart L. Udall Foundation.

There are offices that handle Civil Rights, Child Support Enforcement, Cuba Broadcasting, Economic Adjustment, Elementary and Secondary Education, Environmental Management, Government Ethics, Investor Education and Advocacy, Minority Health, Refugee Resettlement, Science and Technology Policy, and Violence Against Women.

There are services and administrations, including the National Agricultural Statistics Service, National Cemetery Administration, National Constitution Center, National Geospatial-Intelligence Agency, National Interagency Fire Center, National Railroad Passenger Corporation, National

Science Foundation, National Technical Information Service, National Transportation Safety Board, National War College, and National Weather Service.

And don't forget the dozens of standing committees, special committees, select committees, joint committees and subcommittees belonging to the Senate and House of Representatives. If you try to replicate this process for your state, county/parish, and city, it becomes even more impossible to figure out how many governmental bodies are writing laws, rules and regulations, are raising your taxes and assessments, collecting fees and penalties, and otherwise influencing your life.

Is There a Specific Number?

In early January 2020, I called USA.gov to find out just how many federal laws, rules, and regulations there are. I was told to call the Library of Congress, which might have that information. The Library of Congress operator connected me with a researcher, and when I told him I needed to find out how many federal laws, rules, and regulations there are, he replied, "Good luck with that!"

He went on to explain that back in 1982, the Department of Justice commissioned an internal study to determine how many federal criminal laws there were—just *criminal* laws—which turned out to be trickier than it sounds. Some federal criminal laws are located in Title 18 of the United States Code, which can be found online.[14] But many others are embedded in sections of the various federal codes, making it very hard to create a simple, complete list of federal criminal laws. The

[14] See, for example, the Office of the Law Revision Counsel, United States Code, at https://uscode.house.gov/browse/prelim@title18&edition=prelim. Viewed January 14, 2020.

researcher told me that the Justice Department was unable to compile this list of laws, and ended up giving a rough estimate of 3,000 criminal laws.

An interesting article titled "Many Failed Efforts to Count Nation's Federal Criminal Laws,"[15] published in *The Wall Street Journal* in 2011, had this to say about our unknown number of federal criminal laws:

> *For decades, the task of counting the total number of federal criminal laws has bedeviled lawyers, academics and government officials. "You will have died and [been] resurrected three times," and still be trying to figure out the answer, said Ronald Gainer, a retired Justice Department official.*

At the time, in 2011, federal criminal law was "scattered among 50 titles and 23,000 pages of federal law." Since then, more than a few additional laws have been written.

According to the same article, the American Bar Association conducted its own research on the topic in 1998, looking in the federal code for anything related to "fine" and "imprison," plus variations on those words. The article stated that the ABA came to the conclusion that the number of crimes was likely much higher than 3,000, although it couldn't offer a specific number. Whatever the number, some experts estimate that 70% of Americans, or more, have committed a federal crime

---

[15] "Many Failed Efforts to Count Nation's Federal Criminal Laws." By Gary Fields and John R. Emshwiller. *Wall Street Journal*, July 23, 2011. Viewed January 14, 2020. Accessible at https://www.wsj.com/articles/SB10001424052702304319804576389601079728920.

that could land them in jail.[16] Did you know that according to the Code of Federal Regulations, specifically 36 CFR § 2.15 (4), "[a]llowing a pet to make noise that frightens wildlife by barking, howling, or making other noise" is a federal offense?[17] Have you committed this crime, or broken some other law you never knew existed?

If the Justice Department and the American Bar Association can't keep track of our criminal laws, how can we? How can we know which ones we like and which we don't? Which to keep, and which to amend or revoke? Which ones we're violating without even knowing they exist? And which ones are violating our freedom or stealing money from our pockets?

The situation isn't any clearer on the state and local levels. Just try contacting your state senator or representative, your county supervisor, your city mayor or councilperson, and asking for an easy-to-understand list of all the laws, rules, and regulations you have to obey. You probably won't get one.

If no one knows how big our government is, how can we possibly tell if it's efficient and effective? And most importantly, how can we keep it from growing even larger?

Unending Growth

I was scanning the headlines on my computer recently, and the first thing that caught my eye was an article in the *Wall Street*

---

[16] See, for example, "Law Puts Us All in Same Danger as Eric Garner." By Stephen L. Carter. BloombergOpinion, December 4, 2014. Viewed April 9, 2020. Accessible at https://www.bloomberg.com/opinion/articles/2014-12-04/law-puts-us-all-in-same-danger-as-eric-garner.

[17] "36 CFR Ch. 1 (7-1-12 Edition)." GovInfo.gov. Viewed April 9, 2020. Accessible at https://www.govinfo.gov/content/pkg/CFR-2012-title36-vol1/pdf/CFR-2012-title36-vol1-sec2-15.pdf.

Journal announcing, "California Looks to Launch Its Own Prescription-Drug Label."[18]

Health-care expenditures in the United States have reached an all-time high, and prices for many prescription medications have skyrocketed. Health insurance companies have responded by cutting back on the list of medicines they will pay for and, often, charging their customers more. Those who want to buy medications that are *not* on the insurance companies' approved list will find out it's a real budget-buster.

For these reasons, California's Governor Gavin Newsom thinks his state should become a drug company. It would work like this: The state would purchase generic medications directly from pharmaceutical companies, then sell them to the people at affordable rates. Governor Newsom had already ordered California to manage the prescription drug benefits for its 13 million Medicare recipients and to use its market power to negotiate lower prices for the meds. Now Newsom wants to take it a step further. He wants California to launch its own drug label, using its vast population as leverage in the market place.

This might be a well-intentioned idea, but if California goes into the business of buying and selling medicines, the state legislature will have to pass the appropriate laws, which will probably include special favors for some companies. And the state bureaucracy will have to develop all kinds of rules and regulations, plus legal opinions, advisories, and so forth. A new department or agency will have to be created to handle everything. Invariable, California will end up with even more "invisible government" than ever.

---

[18] "California Looks to Launch Its Own Prescription-Drug Label." By Christine Mai-Duc and Jared S. Hopkins. *Wall Street Journal*, Jan. 9, 2020. Viewed January 9, 2020. Accessible at https://www.wsj.com/articles/california-looks-to-launch-its-own-prescription-drug-label-11578578407.

Naturally, money will have to be allocated to support this new bureaucracy, so the state will have to raise taxes or sell more bonds—not a pleasant prospect for Californians, who already hand over large chunks of their paychecks to the government. If not, funds would have to be shifted away from other projects, which will anger those who were supposed to benefit from these projects. Lawsuits will result and, sooner or later, new taxes or fees will be added.

Outside branding experts will have to be hired, at a big fee, to develop a new name and logo for the state drug label, making sure not to offend anyone on the basis of race, religion, actual or preferred gender, citizenship status, cultural appropriation, and more. The state will need to develop a new list of trigger warnings, and new "woke" ways to talk about diseases and drugs that do not offend those belonging to marginalized or previously-discriminated-against groups.

Then the actual buying and selling can begin. Complicated negotiations will have to be conducted between the state and pharmaceutical companies for purchasing the drugs, transporting them, making sure endless rules and regulations are followed, and much more. Naturally, problems will arise, and when they do, the bureaucracy will have to devise even more rules and regulations.

Problems Never End

Let's assume the bureaucracy has been put in place, the money allotted, and everything seems fine. The next big problem for California will be developing its formulary, the official list of medications it will be buying (at a discount) and selling to the public. The state will have to determine which medications Californians typically use, which are medically necessary, which can be substituted for generic brands, which can be purchased at the best price, and so on. Lengthy hearings will be required to create the list, with many economists, citizens, and others weighing in.

No matter which drugs make the list, someone will be unhappy—lots of someones, in fact. People will complain, pressure their representatives, and even sue to get their preferred medicines on the list. Then California will have to deal with other issues. Should medicines for abortions or sex change operations be included on the list? How about vitamins and herbs, and homeopathic medicines? And what of marijuana, used by some cancer patients to help them through chemotherapy and others to relieve stress. Although it's legal to purchase and use marijuana in California, plenty of people would be upset if the state went into the business of buying and selling it.

Then there's the problem of how the state will handle medicines used to treat diseases that affect one group more than another. Elevated blood pressure, for example, is a bigger problem for blacks than it is for Asians, while Tay-Sachs disease most often attacks Ashkenazic Jews. If one group feels that another group is getting more meds, or cheaper ones, you can be sure the case will go all the way to the federal Supreme Court. This, of course, means the State of California will have to spend money beefing up its legal department to handle all of these new complaints and lawsuits.

And what happens when non-Californians want to get in on the deal? After all, the other 290 million other Americans know a good deal when they see it. Servicing the entire country would require a lot more bureaucracy. How about when Canadians try to buy those inexpensive California medicines? Americans have long purchased Canada's lower-priced medicines—isn't turnabout fair play? If California does decide to sell to outsiders, should it charge them more to cover the costs of its bureaucracy and lawsuits? Should there be a system like there is in state universities, with residents paying less than non-residents? And who will make these decisions? How will all this work out?

For clues, we can look to another major project that California undertook in recent years: building a bullet train from San Diego to San Francisco. According to the headline of an article printed in the *Los Angeles Times* in 2019, "Bullet train went from peak California innovation to the project from hell."[19] The article notes that "...huge cost overruns, mismanagement, political concessions and delays ate away at the sleek and soaring vision of a bullet train..." Ten years after it was approved by the voters, the bullet train project is already 13 years behind schedule and has gone $44 billion over its budget.

It's nice that Governor Newsom wants to help his fellow Californians. But adding battalions of bureaucrats, raising taxes, and imposing new laws is not the answer. The solution lies in the free market. And governors govern best when they slash regulation and cut budgets, thereby increasing the power and flexibility of the markets and the people, not decreasing them.

The good news, I suppose, is that if California does get its drug label up and running, it can make a lot of money selling headache remedies to the politicians and bureaucrats beating their heads against a wall while trying to get that bullet train running.

---

[19] "Bullet train went from peak California innovation to the project from hell." By Laura J. Nelson and Joe Mozingo. *Los Angeles Times*, February 14, 2019. Viewed January 9, 2020. Accessible at https://www.latimes.com/local/lanow/la-me-bullet-train-california-problems-20190213-story.html.

Chapter Six

The Candy House of Government Goodies

An old German fairytale tells the story of two children named Hansel and Gretel, who live with their father, a woodcutter, and their stepmother. When a great famine strikes and the parents cannot feed their children, the stepmother urges her husband to abandon the little ones in the forest. Their father reluctantly agrees, even though it breaks his heart. He takes them to the forest and leaves them there.

Hansel and Gretel wander through the forest for hours, growing hungrier and more exhausted by the minute, until they come across what can only be thought of as a miracle. It's a house made entirely of candy! Ravenous, the children start pulling chunks of candy from its walls and gobbling them up. Suddenly, a smiling old woman appears at the front door and invites Hansel and Gretel in for a meal. They happily accept, but as soon as they get inside, they realize the old woman is really a wicked witch. But by then, it's too late. Hansel and Gretel are trapped inside the house, where the wicked witch forces them to do chores from morning until night.

In our modern world, there's a similar "candy house"—the house of government goodies. Instead of candy, it's made of freebies like welfare, tax breaks, federal grants, and the like. Our wicked witch is the government, enticing us into its very appealing house. And we are happy to go inside because we love the free candy. But then we find ourselves trapped and having to jump every time the government snaps its fingers at us. If we don't obey its orders, the flow of goodies will be cut off, so we're afraid to say no. We're stuck, forced to do what the government commands, bending to its will more and more over time. There is no happy ending to this fairytale. The erosion of our freedom just goes on and on.

We all eat from the house of government goodies, every single one of us. Sometimes we do so deliberately, like when we apply for welfare. We might have a very good reason for grabbing the goodies; our children may be hungry, and getting help from the government is the only solution at the moment. Still, we're gobbling government goodies.

Other times, we're enticed into nibbling at the goodies, like when we take tax breaks or rebates. We say to ourselves, "Why *not* take a tax deduction for my home mortgage interest? Why *not* get a rebate from the city for installing energy-efficient windows in the house? Isn't it just free money, waiting to be claimed?" In a certain sense, perhaps you can look at it that way. But it's still getting goodies from the government. And that means there will be a price to pay, sooner or later.

There are still other times when we're force-fed government candy, and truly can't do anything about it. Many states now require that workers must be paid at least $15 per hour. But let's say you are willing to work for $14 an hour. Maybe this lower wage will let you undercut your competition, or maybe it's what performing the job is really worth to the boss. But the government doesn't care about your plan to get ahead, or anyone's opinion of the job's true value. You *must* eat the $15-an-hour candy, like it or not. Unfortunately, this means you might have a lot more trouble finding a job.

There's Never Any "Free Candy"

We're all trapped in the candy house of government goodies to one extent or another. In exchange, we're all forced to do the witches' chores. And she has us doing all kinds of chores, whether as individuals, businesses, charities, universities, or government entities. For example, the federal government gives money to the states to maintain their highways. But at various times, it has used this "gift" to force the states to pass laws to:

- reduce the number of billboards on the interstate system;[20]
- lower the maximum speed limit to 55 miles per hour;
- establish a minimum drinking age of 21;
- require motorcycle riders to wear helmets;
- ban texting while driving.

You may think these are good laws. Then again, you might think that drivers in the wide-open spaces of Wyoming should be allowed to drive faster than those on crowded city streets. Or you might believe that if 19- and 20-year-olds are old enough to join the army and possibly die on foreign soil, they're also old enough to buy themselves some beer. Whatever you feel about these laws, shouldn't you and your fellow citizens be the ones who decide on important issues like these, instead of some far-off government bureaucrats? Be assured that you're not going to be able to make the choice so long as the federal government parcels out the goodies.

---

[20] "Congress's Long And Sordid History Of Handing States Money With Strings Attached." By Merrill Matthews. *Forbes*, August 6, 2014. Viewed January 23, 2020. Accessible at https://www.forbes.com/sites/merrillmatthews/2014/08/06/congresss-long-and-sordid-history-of-handing-states-money-with-strings-attached/#622fea0f4f24.

In 2003, the federal government began providing funds to private groups fighting diseases such as AIDS. But there was a catch. To receive the money, each group would have to adopt a policy opposing sex trafficking and prostitution. AIDS, of course, is a serious, potentially fatal disease that you can catch without being involved in sex trafficking or prostitution. So why should groups fighting AIDS should be forced to take a stand on these issues? Should they also be required to oppose the eating of red meat or endorse the use of sunscreen?

During the rollout of ObamaCare in 2010, the federal government pressured the states to accept a mandatory expansion of Medicaid—that is, the states would have to cover more people under their programs. Naturally, covering more people costs more money. States that refused were threatened with a reduction in the federal funding they received for existing Medicaid. This was a clear case of the federal government demanding that the states do its bidding, or the candy would be withheld.

This happens at the state level, as well. Here in Connecticut, the governor has been fighting hard to push his transportation program through the state legislature. To increase his leverage, he withheld $30 million in aid slated for localities to pay for removing winter snow and trimming trees.[21] The governor was hoping that the cities would respond by pressuring the legislators to agree to his transportation plan. This money is long overdue, putting the localities in a bind. They have to remove the snow, but haven't the money. And they're not in the habit of raising this money themselves. So they have to dance to the tune played by the state fiddler.

[21] "Tows waiting on winter snow removal funds amid bonding stalemate between Gov. Ned Lamont, legislators." By Keith M. Phaneuf. *Hartford Courant*, October 18, 2019. Viewed March 23, 2020. Accessible at https://www.courant.com/politics/hc-pol-lamont-bonding-towns-winter-storms-20191018-onmrbi7ol5bwtkhn3arrj3b5uu-story.html.

We should not be a nation of little Hansels and Gretels, trapped in the house of government goodies, forced to comply with the wicked witch's demands. But that's what happens whenever an individual, organization, city, or state accepts money from the federal government. And the federal government is not the only wicked witch: the state and local governments do the same sort of thing with their own, smaller, houses of government goodies.

We must understand that the government never gives without strings attached; that whatever the government gives, it can take away; and the more we get, the more of our liberty we must relinquish.

The Witch is Also Addicted

As we become more dependent on government candy, the government, in turn, becomes more addicted to the power it has over us. And like any addict, it always wants more, which it often tries to get by passing more laws. Just take a look at the huge amount of new laws that were passed during 2019:

- According to the *Los Angeles Times*, California's "Gov. Gavin Newsome signed almost 1,200 new laws this year [2019]…"[22]
- In New York, "2019 was a historic year. Hundreds of bills were passed after Democratic lawmakers took control of the State Senate…"[23]

[22] "How will California's new laws effect you?" By John Nyers, Priya Krishnahumar, and Phi Do. *Los Angeles Times*, December 27, 2019. Viewed January 7, 2020. Accessible at https://www.latimes.com/projects/new-california-2020-laws/.

[23] "What New Laws Are Coming To New York In 2020." By Sydney Pereira. Gothamist.com, December 30, 2019. Viewed January 7, 2020. Accessible at https://gothamist.com/news/what-new-laws-are-coming-new-york-2020/.

- According to WGEM TV, with the arrival of the new year, "255 new laws are now in effect in Illinois." These laws deal with minimum wage, women's health, hearing aids, the use of the term "locally grown," the teaching of state history in schools, vaccinations for cats, and more—including a requirement that public buildings label single-occupancy bathrooms "restrooms."[24]
- In my state of Connecticut, the legislature recently adopted new laws regarding alcohol, solar panels, e-cigarettes, digital purchases, prepared meals, police training, hearing aids and mental health coverage on insurance policies, and more.[25]

Some of these laws may seem necessary; some may not. But do you even know what they are? Do you know how many new laws and rules and regulations took effect in our country last year? In your state? In your city and county? It's impossible to say. Still, the governmental lawmaking and rulemaking machinery keeps churning them out, while we citizens remain blissfully (and dangerously) unaware.

A Witch on Steroids

What really happens when the government has power over much of your life? Let's look at China, which is providing us with a real-life demonstration. Its government is rolling out a "social credit score" designed to force its citizens to behave exactly the

---

[24] "New Illinois laws for 2020." By Jim Roberts. WGEM, January 1, 2020. Viewed January 5, 2020. Accessible at https://wgem.com/2020/01/01/new-illinois-laws-for-2020/.

[25] "New Connecticut Laws in 2020 That Could Impact Your Life." By Rich Scinto, Patch Staff. January 1, 2020. Viewed January 7, 2020. Accessible at https://patch.com/connecticut/trumbull/new-year-means-new-laws-ct-here-full-list.

way it prescribes. Here's how it works: China has built a high-tech monitoring system that includes over 200 million cameras combined with highly-advanced facial recognition software. These cameras are located on streets, in parks, on subways, and in other public spaces. Everyone begins with a certain social credit score. If a citizen commits any of a number of no-nos, like jaywalking, eating on the subway, or improperly sorting his trash, he can be caught on camera, his face identified, and his score lowered. His score will also be docked if he misses a job interview or a doctor's appointment, spends his money frivolously, fails to show up for a restaurant reservation, goes into debt, or commits any number of other infractions. Those with low scores can improve them by doing things like donating to charity.

If his score drops too low, he'll be put on a list of "Untrustworthy Persons" and punished. Penalties include not being allowed to make reservations at certain hotels, buy high-speed train tickets, or use internet dating sites. Millions of people have already been prevented from purchasing airplane and train tickets or checking into hotels. In addition, their children may not be allowed to attend their desired high schools or colleges, and their employment opportunities may be narrowed. According to *Time Magazine*:

> *In certain areas of China, call a blacklisted person on the phone, and you will hear a siren and recorded message saying: "Warning, this person is on the blacklist. Be careful and urge them to repay their debts."*[26]

---

[26] "How China Is Using 'Social Credit Scores' to Reward and Punish Its Citizens." By Charlie Campbell. *Time*, undated. Viewed January 6, 2020. Accessible at https://time.com/collection/davos-2019/5502592/china-social-credit-score/.

The article also describes how, when people with low scores walk in certain areas of the country's capital city, cameras tied to facial-recognition software will find them and project their images, as well as their ID numbers, on electronic boards so everyone can see the "bad" person.

If, on the other hand, a Chinese citizen has a high social credit score, she will be given preference when applying for a job, discounts when checking into hotels, accelerated approval for travel, and other benefits.

This is not a dystopian fantasy. China has already implemented much of its social credit score system and is working diligently to extend it to every corner of the country. Luckily, we Americans aren't subject to this kind of unrelenting government scrutiny and control—not yet, anyway. But we are being persuaded and forced to surrender more and more of our individual power to the government every day. And history has shown that government doesn't willingly give it back, once it's been gained.

Now, back to Hansel and Gretel, whose story I left unfinished. While the witch was forcing them to do her chores, she continued to feed them very well, which seems like a nice thing to do. In truth, she was fattening them up so she could eat them. But they managed to kill her, discover her hidden treasure, and find their way home. There, they were reunited with their father (the stepmother has passed on), and they live happily ever after.

In real life, our government won't eat us, but it will make us weak and dependent by enticing and trapping us with goodies, then guiding our every action. In the process, it will become more and more powerful. And the more powerful the government becomes, the weaker and less important we become.

They're Eating Your Candy!

Despite all this, you may enjoy munching on candy from the house of government goodies. But how would you feel if you learned that some people were being given more candy than you? And better candy, at that! It turns out that the American government, just like the Chinese, actually does give extra candy to certain favorites. And there's an excellent chance that you're not one of them.

How does this work? The government—federal, state, and local—handles countless functions, from building roads to fighting wars, parceling out Social Security to staffing the courts, running police departments to issuing business licenses. But it doesn't do all of this on its own. Much of the time, it hires non-governmental firms or individuals to do the actual hands-on work. For example, the City of Boston contracted with Bechtel and Parsons Brinckerhoff to oversee an $8 billion highway project known as the "Big Dig."

Contracting out work can be a good way to keep a lid on the size of the permanent government workforce. Once a job is completed, the government simply removes contract workers from the payroll. The problem is that, all too often, the government turns contracts into candy to be used in an attempt to make us all "equal."

Minority Rules & Ladies First

The government doesn't always award contracts to the firms or people offering the best prices, the most expertise, superior reputations, or anything else that makes sense. Instead, it sets aside a certain number of contracts to be awarded to businesses owned by those it considers disadvantaged—such as women,

Black Americans, Native Americans, Hispanic Americans, and others. This means that if I, a white woman, own a street paving business and bid on a government contract, I might have an advantage over a white male competitor because I'm female. At the same time, I might be at a disadvantage if I'm bidding against a Black American, Native American, or Hispanic American woman or man.

The government justifies this blatant discrimination on the grounds that women, Black Americans, Native Americans, Hispanic Americans, LGBTQ Americans, disabled veterans and certain other groups are currently or have been discriminated against because of race, gender, physical disabilities, and other criteria. But their solution, giving these groups an artificial leg up today, continues the practice of discrimination. All they've done is change the victims, with the new targets being those who are white and male. In the process, they are pitting groups against each other and creating resentment by offering more candy to some than to others.

This is not to denigrate firms owned by those who belong to minority or disadvantaged groups. Many of them do a great job and deserve all the contracts they can land. But my firm may also do a great job, yet lose the contract because I'm not part of a disadvantaged group.

If your company was bidding on a contract worth a million or a billion dollars, would you feel it was okay to lose the job to a firm owned by people from a disadvantaged group? Even if your bid was every bit as valid as theirs, or maybe even more so?

Gaming the System

This awarding of contracts partially on the basis of disadvantaged status puts the government in the position of arbitrarily choosing winners and losers—exactly the way it works under communism. Those who belong to the Party get more; those who don't get less, sometimes to the point of getting nothing.

Another problem with giving preferential status to certain groups is it encourages businesses to game the rules. In communist countries, people routinely skirt the rules by bribing someone or getting help from those in power. In the U.S., it's less blatant but still far too common. For example, the owners of a firm may be tempted to grant partial ownership to a person from a disadvantaged group, or put that person on their board of directors, or align with a subcontractor from a disadvantaged group. Any of these steps may allow the firm to claim disadvantaged status.

Other firms actually "rent" people from disadvantaged groups who pretend they are part-owners of the company just long enough to qualify for preference, as in this court case, in which a Boston jury found against:

> *a Chelmsford, Massachusetts man who won over $100 million in federal contracts that gave preference to disabled veteran-owned companies, finding that he... recruited two veterans to stand in as the majority owners and top executives of his construction firm so it could win those federal contracts.*[27]

You might think this unequal distribution of government candy is wonderful for the disadvantaged. But does it really

[27] "Fraud in Connection With Contract Preferences or Set-Asides for Small Businesses or Businesses Owned by Veterans, Service-Disabled Veterans, Women or Disadvantaged Minorities, Part II." No author listed. Berger/Montague, undated. Viewed January 10, 2020. Accessible at https://bergermontague.com/small-business-contractor-false-claims-part-2/.

help them in the long run? Does it force their firms to become more efficient, effective, and innovative so they can beat out the competition? Or does it allow them to slide by on their status, all the while stirring up a lot of resentment and encouraging people to game the system?

Minority Confusion

Making matters more confusing, it's not always clear what constitutes a minority or member of a disadvantaged group. For example, if one of your grandparents belonged to a minority group, do you qualify? How about one of your great-grandparents? Or does it only matter how you decide to identify yourself? Often, the answer is subjective. If you are one-eight African American and seven-eights white, yet identify as being black, do you qualify as a minority?

Suppose you belong to a group that your state recognizes as a Native American tribe, but the federal government does not? Yes, this happens. In recent cases, over $500 million worth of contracts were awarded to companies owned by people the federal government regarded as having no Native American ancestry or recognition.[28]

And what happens if you make an honest mistake—or at least you say it's an honest mistake? Senator Elizabeth Warren of Massachusetts has long claimed to be part Native American, based on family lore. But when she finally had her DNA analyzed, the evidence was weak. At best, the most recent Native American in her family tree appears six to ten

[28] "Two tribes aren't recognized federally. Yet members won $500 million in minority contracts." By Adam Elmahrek and Paul Pringle. *Los Angeles Times*, January 1, 2020. Page A1. Viewed January 12, 2020. Accessible at https://www.latimes.com/california/story/2019-12-31/native-american-tribes-alabama-minority-contracts.

generations ago.[29] Warren herself has never lived on tribal land, was never enrolled in a tribal group, and doesn't speak a Native American language. So is she really a Native American, or just a woman who happens to possess a tiny bit of the "right" kind of DNA?

As if all this isn't confusing enough, how should the government deal with people who suddenly discover they are members of a disadvantaged group? According to a 2018 article[30] printed in the *Seattle Times*, a man named Ralph Taylor, who lived his entire life as a white man and identified himself accordingly, took a home DNA test. The results showed that he was 90% European, 6% Indigenous American, and 4% Sub-Saharan African. Based on this, Taylor decided that he was actually "multi-racial." And because he owned an insurance agency, it qualified as a minority-owned enterprise that should get preferential status when considered for government contracts.

Because there are no hard-and-fast rules defining who is and who is not a minority, the Washington State Office of Minority & Women's Business Enterprises approved Taylor's request for state certification as multi-racial. But this very same state agency, which also handles requests for certification with the U.S. Department of Transportation, turned Taylor down for certification as a Federal Disadvantaged Business Enterprise. According to the federal rules, they decided, he was white. So he's multi-racial at the state level of government, white at federal.

---

[29] "The Facts on Elizabeth Warren's DNA Test." By Jessica McDonald. FactCheck.org, October 30, 2018. Viewed January 10, 2020. Accessible at https://www.factcheck.org/2018/10/the-facts-on-elizabeth-warrens-dna-test/.

[30] "Lynnwood man tried to use a home DNA test to qualify as a minority business owner. He was denied – now he's suing." By Christine Willmsen. *Seattle Times*, September 13, 2018. Viewed January 13, 2020. Accessible at https://www.seattletimes.com/seattle-news/lynnwood-man-tried-to-use-a-home-dna-test-to-qualify-as-a-minority-business-owner-he-was-denied-now-hes-suing/.

What can a business owner do in such a situation? He can sue, which is exactly what Mr. Taylor did. He went to court demanding the right to be treated as a minority where federal contracts are concerned. The 9th U.S. Circuit Court of Appeals is currently considering his case.

In short, Mr. Taylor was raised white, could not produce any evidence of being Native American or black, or identifying with either group, until he got his DNA test results, when he was well into his fifties. Neither could he produce any evidence of being discriminated against for being Native American or black at any time during his life. Yet he is now in federal court, suing for the right to be considered non-white.

Total Insanity

Why is the government giving preference to certain groups? Why are they picking winners and losers solely on the basis of race, gender, sexual identification, and similar criteria?

We've been pushing for decades to move away from a society in which one group gets preferential treatment over another. Yet, with this system of preferential contracting, we are promoting and prolonging this behavior. The only thing that has changed is that different groups now fall into the categories of winners and losers. In a society where *all* are supposed to have a voice in the government, be colorblind, and learn to live together, shouldn't the government abstain from driving wedges between various groups? Don't we realize that turning societal groups against each other is one of the oldest and most successful tricks in the communist playbook?

Chapter Seven

I Love Hate America!

The Worcester Art Museum outside of Boston, Massachusetts is a gem of a museum, well worth a visit. Its wonderful collection of 18th and 19th century American Art, beginning before the revolution and continuing through the Civil War, includes paintings by famous artists like Gilbert Stuart, Winslow Homer, and John Singleton Copley.

Unfortunately, in 2018, the museum decided to join the campaign to turn Americans against America. Beating the drums of "historical accuracy" and "restoring Blacks to history," it put labels next to portraits of certain early Americans, identifying them as slave owners or otherwise beneficiaries of America's "peculiar institution" (slavery). Slavery is one of America's ugly truths. But what's also ugly is seeing slavery highlighted in a manner designed—deliberately or inadvertently—to drive wedges between us.

Up until now, the purpose of labels on the walls next to works of art has been to offer information about the artist, who or what the work represents, the materials used in its creation, and so on. These new labels add new information, but in a *gotcha!* sort of way. "You can't fool us," they proclaim. "Don't try to hide behind your powdered wig and pretty clothes. We know you owned slaves, or participated somehow in the slave trade, or otherwise became wealthy in an economy that profited from slave labor, even if you had no direct connection to slavery."

As one of the wall labels at the museum explains: "These paintings depict the sitters as they wish to be seen—their best selves …",[31] meaning the paintings don't show the sitters with their slaves, assuming they had any, or otherwise behaving in dastardly ways. I don't know about you, but I suspect that people paying large fees to VIP artists to paint their portraits would want to be presented in a pleasing manner. Would you hire an artist to paint an ugly picture of yourself, showing all the stupid and cruel things you've done? Would you hang that on your wall and invite your friends over to see it?

The museum claims that these labels are designed to reveal the full truth about those in the portraits. If so, how about labels that also describe how much money these people donated to charity, or whether they took up arms in defense of their country, or helped establish a local library or school?

Or, assuming the museum only wants to emphasize the negative sides of the portrait sitters, why not add labels about them being tax cheats? Many of the revolutionary figures whose portraits hang in museums dodged or encouraged the dodging of taxes that were lawfully levied by their ruler, King George III. Some even physically attacked royal tax collectors and illegally dumped tea in Boston Harbor to protest having to pay tax. Or how about adding labels that call out the sitters for being anti-Semitic or anti-Catholic? The majority of early Americans were Protestants, and most disliked Jews and Catholics to one degree or another. Jews and Catholics were barred from many professions and social associations, although they generated business and taxes that enriched the nation as a whole.

---

[31] "A Massachusetts Museum Is Taking a New Approach to Wall Text: Revealing Early American Portrait Sitters With Ties to Slavery." By Sarah Cascone. *ArtNews.net*, June 19, 2018. Viewed January 23, 2020. Accessible at https://news.artnet.com/exhibitions/worcester-art-museum-slavery-wall-text-1305407.

If the point of adding these "you miserable jerk" labels next to certain people's portraits was to improve society today by outing the folks of yesteryear, the Worcester Art Museum has failed. These labels can certainly provoke anger and outrage, claim that our history is an evil lie, and encourage us to loathe our country and ourselves (if we're white). But they can also accentuate divisions, rather than draw us together. They can encourage a victim mentality in some, while prodding others to hate themselves for the sins of their very distant ancestors—assuming they had ancestors in this country way back then. But these labels do not help us move forward. That's because they're about a past that cannot be changed, rather than a future waiting to be written.

If the Worcester Art Museum truly wants to improve society, why not take a positive approach? Perhaps they could commission artists to paint new portraits of individual Blacks and Black families of the 17th and 18th centuries, and create scenes of the period from the Black perspective. Some of these pictures would be pleasing to look at while others would be painful, showing the awful truth of slavery. They would depict history as it was, and invite us to contemplate the evil effects of slavery without beating us over the head with the assertion that "American history is a lie and its all-white heroes were terrible people."

This museum (or others) might also consider creating an exhibition of existing paintings of Blacks and Black life from the 17th and 18th centuries that could travel to museums and other exhibition sites all over the country. Charles Wilson Peale's "Portrait of Yarrow Mamout (Muhammad Yaro)," painted in 1819 and now in the Philadelphia Museum of Art, would be an excellent piece to include in the exhibition.

Either of these approaches would remind Americans that we have come a long way. They would prompt us to wonder whether we have completed our journey to a country where we are judged by the content of our character, not the color of our skin. Rather than dividing us into "good" and "bad" people, they would encourage us to work together toward this great goal.

But we probably won't see things like this happen. That's because the mania for rewriting American history that has swept the country in recent years is more about inflaming than healing wounds, more about separating than bringing us together.

The "New" History of Our Country

History is continually revised as new facts are discovered and old knowledge is reinterpreted. That can be a good thing, especially if the process is driven by historians with a firm grasp on facts old and new. But the current wave of reinterpreting history seems specifically designed to denigrate our country, its ideals, and many of the people we have held up as heroes.

Today, especially in college, students are often taught that:

- The Founding Fathers were Awful White Men who owned slaves and suppressed women, rather than great (if flawed) men with a vision of a better future.
- Christopher Columbus was a horrible human being, and all positive mention of him should be erased.
- The tremendous sacrifices the U.S. has made to defeat Nazism and Communism don't really count because "capitalism profits from war."

- European and American art is just a bunch of sexist, racist, and worthless "dead white man" stuff.
- If history conflicts with how certain groups are feeling today, it should be obliterated.
- People have the right to demand every single liberty they can think of, and should not waste much time thinking about what they owe to others and to society in return.
- Our country is irredeemably racist, sexist, ageist, and every other evil "ist" you can think of. It can only be "saved" by continually bringing up the terrible sins of the past and loudly harping on every real or imagined problem that arises today, no matter how small or inadvertent it may be. And we must keep slamming away at this until all who believe in the essential goodness of America are beaten into submission and will confess their sins.

This new history is rarely nuanced. It pays little regard to the fact that ideas evolve over time, and we can't judge the past solely by the standards of the present. Neither is there an acknowledgment that while we've made serious mistakes, and continue to do so, we've also made tremendous strides in creating a fair and open society. Instead, we all seem to be encouraged to despise our country and, depending on the group you belong to, either loudly proclaim your grievances and demand change, or beat your breast in shame, or just keep your head down and hope your life isn't destroyed if you make some little verbal or Twitter slip.

Being Taught to Hate America

There is no single course on "Hating America" that we are all forced to sit through. Instead, it's a multipronged process, occurring in both obvious and subtle ways. But make no mistake, it's happening in our arts, politics, schools, and other arenas.

Think of the way many politicians and thought leaders talk about our country. For example, at a meeting of immigrants and refugees, former Texas Congressman Beto O'Rourke, a candidate for the 2020 Democratic presidential nomination, proclaimed: "This country was founded on white supremacy. And every single structure that we have in this country still reflects the legacy of slavery and segregation and Jim Crow and suppression."[32]

Statements like this not only exaggerate the negative, but also encourage people with grievances to pin their hatred on the country. To look back in anger, with eyes firmly fixed on those evil people who created this "hellhole." And on those who look like them today.

The media plays a major role in teaching us to despise ourselves and our past. One of the best examples of this is an ongoing effort by *The New York Times Magazine* called the "1619 Project" that "aims to reframe the country's history by placing the consequences of slavery and the contributions of black Americans at the very center of our national narrative."[33]

---

[32] "Woke assimilation: Teaching our politicians to hate America." By Rich Lowry. *New York Post*, July 15, 2019. Viewed January 25, 2020. Accessible at https://nypost.com/2019/07/15/woke-assimilation-teaching-our-politicians-to-hate-america/.

[33] "The 1619 Project." *New York Times Magazine*. Viewed January 25, 2020. Accessible at https://www.nytimes.com/interactive/2019/08/14/magazine/1619-america-slavery.html.

In other words, everything about our history now has to do with Blacks and slavery.

The New York Times Magazine stated in its lead article for the "1619 Project" that our Founding Fathers only rebelled against England to protect slavery.[34] Unfortunately for the *Times*, the lead article contained errors and tortured interpretations, and it has been called to task by historians.[35] These historians point out that slavery was firmly ensconced in America and other British colonies, and people back then did not fear it would be eliminated any time soon, if at all. But that doesn't matter to those who insist that this country is irredeemably evil. They *know* they are right, and will keep repeating their distortions until they are accepted as fact.

College Versus the USA

College professors are some of the worst culprits when it comes to teaching young Americans to disdain America. Professor Charles Angeletti, for example, of the Metropolitan State University of Denver, who teaches a course in American Civilization, believes the U.S. is intolerant, repressive, racist, and heavily Christian-oriented. So he asked his students to recite this pledge:

[34] "Our democracy's founding ideals were false when they were written. Black Americans have fought to make them true." By Nikole Hannah-Jones. *New York Times Magazine*, August 14, 2019. Viewed January 25, 2020. Accessible at https://www.nytimes.com/interactive/2019/08/14/magazine/black-history-american-democracy.html.

[35] "A Matter of Facts." By Sean Wilentz. *Atlantic*, January 22, 2020. Viewed January 25, 2020. Accessible at https://www.theatlantic.com/ideas/archive/2020/01/1619-project-new-york-times-wilentz/605152/. See also "1619 Project Fact-Checker Says *The New York Times* Ignored Her Objections." By Robby Soave. *Reason*, March 6, 2020. Viewed March 21, 2020. Accessible at https://reason.com/2020/03/06/1619-project-fact-checker-nikole-hannah-jones-leslie-harris/.

I pledge allegiance to and wrap myself in the flag of the United States Against Anything Un-American. And to the Republicans for which it stands, two nations, under Jesus, rich against poor, with curtailed liberty and justice for all except blacks, homosexuals, women who want abortions, Communists, welfare queens, treehuggers, feminazis, illegal immigrants, children of illegal immigrants, and you, if you don't watch your step.[36]

Concerning the 9/11 attacks, Professor Haunani-Kay Trask of the University of Hawaii said:

Why should we support the United States, whose hands are soaked with blood?... The enemy is the United States of America and everyone who supports it.[37]

Statements like these can be found all over the media and social networks. But college professors, who are in the business of educating and molding young minds, can be especially effective in turning students against our country. An example of this is the "New Civics" course of study that is starting to appear in major colleges and universities. Civics courses were originally designed to teach students the essential facts about the government, the Constitution, the rights and duties

---

[36] "College prof makes students recite anti-American 'pledge of allegiance.'" Fox News, December 8, 2014. Last updated November 30, 2015. Viewed January 24, 2020. Accessible at https://www.foxnews.com/us/college-prof-makes-students-recite-anti-american-pledge-of-allegiance.

[37] Horowitz, David. **The Professors: The 101 Most Dangerous Academics in America**. Simon & Schuster, 2006. P344.

of citizenship, and so on. But the New Civics, according to the National Association of Scholars:

> *... seeks above all to make students into enthusiastic supporters of the New Left's dream of "fundamentally transforming" America. The transformation includes de-carbonizing the economy, massively redistributing wealth, intensifying identity group grievance, curtailing the free market, expanding government bureaucracy, elevating international "norms" over American Constitutional law, and disparaging our common history and ideals.*[38]

In other words, the New Civics seeks to turn students into socialists! This idea undoubtedly finds favor among many professors, who are overwhelmingly Democratic. A recent study looked at the faculty members of 51 liberal-arts colleges to see how many were registered Democrats versus registered Republicans. The study found that faculty members are much more likely to be Democrats than Republicans, with Democrats-to-Republicans ratios of:

- 70:1 in religion;
- 21:1 in biology;
- 17:1 in history, philosophy, and psychology;
- 8:1 in political science;
- 6:1 in economics, mathematics, and physics;
- 5:1 in chemistry.

[38] "Making Citizens: How American Universities Teach Civics." National Association of Scholars, January 2017. Viewed January 25, 2020. Accessible at https://www.nas.org/storage/app/media/Reports/Making%20Citizens/NAS_makingCitizens_fullReport.pdf.

The study noted that there was not a single field of study "in which Republicans are more numerous than Democrats."[39]

This doesn't mean that all Democratic professors are trying to turn students into socialists, but there is an excellent chance that their political leanings influence what they decide to teach and how they present the material. The combination of left-leaning politics, distortion of the facts, and New Civics can make a particularly strong impression on young, impressionable minds. That's especially true because many students (and most Americans, in general) are fairly ignorant about our country's history. For example, the 2019 Annenberg Civics Knowledge Survey found that less than 40% of Americans were able to name the three branches of the federal government.[40] And a survey by the Woodrow Wilson National Fellowship Foundation[41] asked 1,000 Americans to answer 20 multiple choice questions about American history, taken from the practice exam for the U.S. Citizenship Test. The results were dismal, leading one writer to ask:

> *So what do we do when only 13 percent of Americans know when the U.S. Constitution was ratified? Or when six in 10 don't know which countries the United States fought in*

---

39 "The problem with all those liberal professors." By Cass R. Sunstein. *Chicago Tribune*, September 24, 2018. Viewed January 25, 2020. Accessible at https://www.chicagotribune.com/opinion/commentary/ct-perspec-professors-liberal-teaching-students-colleges-universities-0925-story.html.

40 "Annenberg Civics Knowledge Survey." No author given. Annenberg Public Policy Centerm undated. Viewed January 25, 2020. Accessible at https://www.annenbergpublicpolicycenter.org/political-communication/civics-knowledge-survey/.

41 "National Survey Finds Just 1 In 3 Americans Would Pass Citizenship Test." Woodrow Wilson National Fellowship Foundation press release, October 3, 2018. Viewed January 25, 2020. https://woodrow.org/news/national-survey-finds-just-1-in-3-americans-would-pass-citizenship-test/.

> *World War II? Or when less than a quarter of Americans know why we fought the British during the Revolutionary War?*[42]

We don't all have to be scholars of American history. But it is clear that those who know this little are easy prey for those with an agenda, especially if they happen to be your professors.

Selling Out History for a Buck

It's not just colleges and universities that are big on rewriting history. Businesses are now jumping into the fray. For example, in 2019, Nike introduced a red, white, and blue sneaker with a picture of the Betsy Ross flag on its heel to celebrate the 4th of July. The flag had thirteen stars, representing the original thirteen states, arranged in a circle on a field of blue. This is a famous image we've probably all seen in history textbooks, on flagpoles at patriotic celebrations, or on TV documentaries. I wouldn't be surprised to learn that some clever people have figured out how to paint the Betsy Ross flag in the night sky with fireworks.

Unfortunately, certain hate groups, including the KKK, have used this flag as a symbol. Just as unfortunately, Nike yanked the patriotic shoe when Colin Kaepernick called it offensive, connecting it to an era when Blacks were enslaved. Kaepernick, formerly an NFL quarterback, is a Nike brand ambassador. The shoe company announced that Nike was halting distribution of the sneaker "based on concerns that

[42] "When it comes to knowledge of American history, we are a nation at risk." By Arthur Levine. *The Hill*, October 17, 2018. Viewed January 25, 2020. Accessible at https://thehill.com/opinion/education/411700-when-it-comes-to-knowledge-of-american-history-we-are-a-nation-at-risk.

it could unintentionally offend and detract from the nation's patriotic holiday."[43]

I wonder if Nike's thinking wasn't really based on the bucks, as in: "We'll appeal to a lot of customers—the ones who don't like America—by dropping this shoe. We'll sell enough of our other shoes to these same people to make up for the bad publicity."

If that's what they were thinking, they're cowards. Nike is one of the major shoe companies in the nation, with a worldwide presence. Why didn't they stand up for our country? Why didn't they proudly announce they were helping to restore the flag to its rightful place in the American story? Why didn't they shout from the rooftops that they want to protect America, rather than running for cover at the slightest whiff of controversy?

When Nike brought Kaepernick on as a brand ambassador, they proudly unveiled a new slogan: "Believe in something, even if it means sacrificing everything." So what does Nike believe in, and what is it willing to sacrifice to protect our history?

A Plea for History

We need our history! A unifying history that proudly proclaims our principles, highlights those who made the U.S. the greatest nation in the world, and examines those who, at times, brought it low. And we need a powerful unifying principle. Monarchies have their royalty, ethnic nations have their shared genes, and other nations have their common religious beliefs to bind them

---

[43] "Nike Drops 'Betsy Ross Flag' Sneaker After Kaepernick Criticizes It." By Tiffany Hsu, Kevin Draper, Sandra E. Garcia, and Niraj Chokshi. *New York Times*, July 2, 2019. Viewed January 28, 2020. Accessible at https://www.nytimes.com/2019/07/02/business/betsy-ross-shoe-kaepernick-nike.html.

together. Unifying principles such as these can give nations a common "language," a common set of ideas and hopes, a shared vision of the future.

We don't have these kinds of unifying elements in the United States. Many of us are immigrants, and many do not speak English. There is a wide range of religious beliefs practiced in this country. We cannot rally around our beloved monarchy—the Kardashians don't qualify—and we cannot call ourselves an ethnic group. Our gene pool likely incudes people from every single other nation and group on the planet.

We lack the glue that holds so many other countries together. But what we do have is the Constitution and Declaration of Independence. We have the Founding Fathers who created our nation, the abolitionists who spurred its recreation via the bloody Civil War, and the immigrants of all kinds of who have continually brought eager hands and fresh ideas to the country. We have the shared belief that everyone should be free to enjoy life, liberty, and the pursuit of happiness. We have public monuments to heroes like the Rev. Martin Luther King and the soldiers who raised the American flag at Iwo Jima. We have paintings and artworks that take us back to various times in our history. But most of all, we have our common desire for a better future, plus the shared faith that it *will* be better.

But if we allow others to take away our history, they will also take away our sense of who we are and what we aspire to be.

If our history is replaced with a narrative based on self-hatred and grievances, the chances that our country will fracture along racial, economic, demographic, and other lines greatly increase.

If our history disappears, so will the ideals our nation was founded on, ideals that can propel us into a better future and that should belong to everyone.

We shouldn't let *anyone* rewrite the story of where we've been, what we've done, and what we aspire to be. If that happens, we will have lost our national soul. Just ask anyone who lived in Czechoslovakia before 1989. They know.

P.S. If we're really interested in absolute historical accuracy and revealing all the nasty things about our heroes, shouldn't the official portrait of President Bill Clinton, the one hanging in the White House, have a little picture of Monica Lewinsky next to it?

Chapter Eight

Spitting on Speech

In communist Czechoslovakia, you had to watch your words carefully. You could never criticize the government openly, and just making the "wrong" offhand comment could get you hauled off to the local police station for a stern talking-to. If what you said was expressly forbidden, you might just find yourself demoted to a lesser job, unemployed, or even tossed in jail.

The power of the Communist Party was weakening as I entered my teens, so people my age pushed against governmental boundaries in ways our parents would never even have dreamed of. It sounds like nothing today; things like refusing to call our teachers "comrade," listening to the songs of banned protest singers like Karel Kryl, and watching pirated tapes of Western movies.

Yet even young, rebellious people knew not to talk about politics, unless they were at home. It still wasn't safe to speak freely about such things, and you never knew if someone who happened to overhear you might be a government informant. Speaking your mind to a good friend was also risky because your friend might repeat what you said to someone else, who turned out to be an informer.

Even at home, we couldn't speak openly in the kitchen, the bathroom, and the toilet. (In the standard Czechoslovakian apartment, the bathtub was in one room, the toilet in another.) In truth, these places might have been the least private areas of the house. A central vent for the entire building passed through the kitchen, making it a great place to plant a listening device. And bathrooms and toilets had pipes and vents that amplified sound and passed it directly into the ears of anyone listening. The best place for secret conversations was a closet, although that could have been bugged.

Luckily, we don't have this problem in the U.S., thanks to the First Amendment, a constitutional guarantee that we can speak our minds. This means that if I want to, I can publicly declare that a certain politician is a total idiot. I can put a sign on my lawn proclaiming my allegiance to one candidate without fear that if the other candidate wins, I'll be thrown in jail. Of course, I can't yell "fire" in a crowded theatre or libel someone without fear of legal consequences. But in general, I can speak my mind without fear of repercussions.

At least, that's what I thought in 1988 when I first came to the U.S. Since that time, I've learned that although the First Amendment says the government can't prohibit your right to speak, you still have to be *very careful* about what you say, write, or do, or you may find yourself on the wrong side of the politically correct crowd.

Many years ago, the phrase "politically correct" (PC) meant being politically wise. In the 1970s, the term was used by members of the political left to poke fun at other leftists they thought were overly serious and rigid in their political philosophies. But PC has since come to mean something entirely different: the scrutinizing of our language, behavior, policies, activities, and even our thoughts, intending to eliminate any expression or action that seems to exclude, marginalize or insult groups of people who are discriminated against or socially disadvantaged.

The penalty for stepping over one of these imaginary PC lines is being attacked (verbally) by angry "victims" and righteous observers. The attack can lead to public embarrassment, loss of your job, and more. Yet, in truth, political correctness is often totally subjective. It's just someone's rigid and, quite often, ridiculous standard of "right" and "wrong" language/behavior/thoughts that is being forced on us by a group of supposedly virtuous people. And as they dictate the "proper" ways for us to express ourselves, they are whittling away at our right to free speech. After all, if you're afraid to speak up, write something, donate to certain causes, or go to certain meetings or other places, it doesn't matter what the First Amendment says—you don't enjoy truly free speech.

Free Speech – What America Is All About

The Founding Fathers understood the vital importance of freedom of speech, knowing that a free nation can only flourish when people can freely exchange ideas, question each other, challenge each other, insult each other, and offend the hell out of each other. And they must be able to do these things verbally, in print, and in groups. That's why the First Amendment to the U.S. Constitution prohibits the federal government from "abridging the freedom of speech, or of the press; or of the right of the people peaceably to assemble..."

Without free speech, Frederick Douglas and William Lloyd Garrison could not have challenged slavery in America openly.

Without free speech, Susan B. Anthony would not have been able to give speeches across the country, promoting and insisting on the right to vote for women.

Without free speech, books like Walt Whitman's **Leaves of Grass** and Ernest Hemingway's **The Sun Also Rises** might never have been published. (Have you ever heard the expression, "banned in Boston?" Whitman and Hemingway did.)

Without free speech, students protesting the Vietnam War would not have been allowed to march in protests or wear black armbands to school.

Without free speech, Martin Luther King would not have been able to stand on the steps of the Lincoln Memorial in Washington, D.C. and proclaim to the world, "I have a dream!"

At the time, millions of people were outraged by these ideas and behaviors; they felt they were being insulted and (figuratively) spat upon. They felt that their place in the world and their understanding of it was threatened by them. Yet, American history has shown that offensive speech, offensive writing, and offensive assembly are key elements of the democratic process. Think of the Declaration of Independence, which, at the time, was incredibly offensive to the government in power. In it, the colonists accused King George III of obstructing justice, conducting mock trials, passing destructive laws, suborning judges, and much more. They asserted that "He has plundered our seas, ravaged our Coasts, burnt our towns, and destroyed the lives of our people."[44] If that's not offensive, what is? Yet it is exactly what the United States was founded upon, grew strong upon, and is now at risk of losing.

Free Speech Versus Hate Speech

Even though the Constitution and the federal government continue to protect freedom of speech, press, and assembly, they are under assault from the very people they are designed to protect: U.S. citizens. You can see this in a 2019 poll of

---

[44] "Declaration of Independence: A Transcription." National Archives. Viewed February 1, 2020. Accessible at https://www.archives.gov/founding-docs/declaration-transcript.

slightly over 1,000 Americans, performed by Campaign for Free Speech,[45] which found that:

- 61% of Americans believe it is time to put restrictions on free speech.
- 51% feel that the First Amendment has outlived its usefulness and should be replaced.
- 57% feel the government should be empowered to go after TV stations and newspapers that offend.
- 48% feel that "hate speech" should be made illegal.

The last item takes us to the heart of the matter and explains why so many people want to jettison one of our most basic freedoms: they are concerned about "hate speech."

Dictionaries define hate speech as utterances that demonstrate hatred toward a person or group because of some attributes, such as sexual orientation, race, or religion. Hate speech may also encourage violence. I don't like the idea of people spewing hate at each other, and I certainly don't want people harming each other. But have the promoters of political correctness reached this reasonable bar? No. Instead, they have pushed the bar down as low as it can go, turning the smallest statement, gesture, or action into a cause for righteous indignation. These tiny actions are called *microaggressions,* examples of alleged hatred that are so small you need a microscope to find them.

You can easily see the absurdity of microaggression at our nation's universities, where political correctness seems to have an iron grip. One of our premier educational institutions, the

[45] "Majority of Americans Want to Scrap First Amendment, Polling Finds." by Free Speech Team. Campaign for Free Speech, October 23, 2019. Viewed February 1, 2020. Accessible at https://www.campaignforfreespeech.org/free-speech-under-dire-threat-polling-finds/.

University of California, has promulgated a document, a guide titled "Tool: Recognizing Microaggressions and the Messages They Send."[46] According to this document, if you say to a person of color, "When I look at you, I don't see color," or "There is only one race, the human race," or "America is a melting pot," you have committed the microaggression sin of "Color Blindness." This means you are a white person who neither wants nor needs to recognize race. Apparently, according to the University of California, white people should focus intently on another person's race, so they aren't denying the other person as a racial/cultural being. In other words, they should obsess over race, which is the exact opposite of what we've been trying to do for years. Hmmm. Suppose an Asian-American says, "When I look at you, I don't see color." Is that aggressive, in a micro way?

The guide also asserts that it's a microaggression to say, "I'm not racist. I have several Black friends." This is a microaggression called "Denial of Individual Racism/Sexism/Heterosexism." But suppose you are *not* racist and you *do* have several Black friends? Isn't that what we want to see, whites befriending blacks, blacks befriending whites, and members of all groups befriending members of all other groups? Doesn't this "Denial of Individual Racism/Sexism/Heterosexism" guideline tell us that our great goal of loving each other is impossible? And that befriending people who are not like you makes you a racist/sexist/heterosexist and all sorts of other "ists" currently existing or yet to be invented?

Oddly enough, engaging in "hate speech" against whites seems to be a lesser crime. When Sarah Jeong, an Asian

[46] "Tool: Recognizing Microaggressions and the Messages They Send." The University of California, Santa Cruz. Viewed February 1, 2020. Accessible at https://academicaffairs.ucsc.edu/events/documents/Microaggressions_Examples_Arial_2014_11_12.pdf.

American, was hired as a member of the *New York Times* editorial board in 2017, people pointed out that in 2014 and 2015 she had tweeted some pretty nasty things about white people,[47] including:

> *"Oh man it's kind of sick how much joy I get out of being cruel to old white men."*
>
> *"Dumbass f---ing white people marking up the internet with their opinions like dogs pissing on fire hydrant."*
>
> *"Are white people genetically predisposed to burn faster in the sun, thus logically being only fit to live underground like groveling goblins?"*

This sounds awfully hateful to me. Not just microaggressive, but super, kick-in-the-groin aggressive! But, it turns out that I'm wrong. Ms. Jeong, claiming she had simply engaged in "satire," apologized and was allowed to keep her prestigious job. The *New York Times* supported her by saying she had been the "subject of frequent online harassment" and that "for a period of time she responded to that harassment by imitating the rhetoric of her harassers."[48] Apparently, the *New York Times*

---

[47] You can find these quotes at various internet sites. See, for example, "Sarah Jeong out at New York Times editorial board." By Joe Concha. *The Hill*, September 28, 2019. Viewed February 1, 2020. Accessible at https://thehill.com/homenews/media/463503-sarah-jeong-out-at-new-york-times-editorial-board. See also "New York Times racism row: how Twitter comes back to haunt you." By Sam Wolfson. *The Guardian*, August 3, 2018. Viewed April 9, 2020. Accessible at https://www.theguardian.com/technology/2018/aug/03/sarah-jeong-new-york-times-twitter-posts-racism.

[48] "NY Times defends hiring editorial writer after emergence of past racial tweets." By Joe Concha. *The Hill*, August 2, 2018. Viewed February 2, 2020. Accessible at https://thehill.com/homenews/

believes it's okay to spew hatred as long as you're doing so in the name of retaliation, and you're not white.

This is just a taste of the PC insanity that has swept across the nation, invading educational institutes, businesses, clubs, and even the government. It threatens to weaken or wreck our legal rights to free speech, freedom of the press, and freedom of assembly in favor of trying to ensure no one from a disadvantaged group ever feels offended by "hate speech."

And yet there is no rational, objective standard for "hate speech"—it's all in the ears of the beholder. What the speaker actually meant is not important; the only thing that matters is what the listener *feels* about what was said or done. There is no single standard to which all are held, no matter what their race, creed, or color. It's a subjective and dangerous game, one that threatens to do away with our First Amendment rights. And it's being played with deadly seriousness.

Pilloried by PC

Is the PC threat really that serious? Just ask Bret Weinstein, who teaches biology at Washington's Evergreen State College. Mr. Weinstein, a liberal who supported the Occupy Wall Street movement and is a fan of Senator Bernie Sanders, stepped on a PC landmine when he spoke out against his college's "Day of Absence."

A tradition dating back to the 1970s, the Day of Absence is a day for students and faculty of color to skip class and meet off-campus. The idea is to show, by their absence, how important people of color are to the university. Then, in 2017, the college decided to reverse things, with white students and

---

media/400121-ny-times-defends-hiring-of-editorial-writer-after-emergence-of-past-racial.

faculty staying off-campus for the day. According to the *New York Times*, "The decision was made after students of color 'voiced concern over feeling as if they are unwelcome on campus, following the 2016 election'."[49] That's the one in which Donald Trump was elected president.

Mr. Weinstein thought this was a case of "moral bullying" because the white students were told to stay off-campus as a kind of punishment because the students of color weren't feeling welcome. It wasn't the same thing as the students and faculty of color deciding to take the day off, as a statement. Weinstein made his opinion known, was accosted by several dozen angry students on campus and, according to the *New York Times*:

> *The video of that exchange... must be seen to be believed. It will make anyone who believes in the liberalizing promise of higher education quickly lose heart....*[50]

Under orders from the college president to back off, the college police told Mr. Weinstein that they couldn't protect him on campus, and he was forced to hold his class in a park. These angry PC protests have been repeated at universities across the country, and have sometimes become violent, as noted in the *Washington Post*:

> *...at the University of Virginia, the College of William & Mary and the University of California*

---

[49] "When the Left Turns on Its Own." By Bari Weiss. *New York Times*, June 1, 2017. Viewed February 1, 2020. Accessible at https://www.nytimes.com/2017/06/01/opinion/when-the-left-turns-on-its-own.html.

[50] "When the Left Turns on Its Own." By Bari Weiss. *New York Times*, June 1, 2017. Viewed February 1, 2020. Accessible at https://www.nytimes.com/2017/06/01/opinion/when-the-left-turns-on-its-own.html.

> *at Berkeley, among others... appearances by controversial speakers resulted in protests with armed police officers reminiscent of a war zone, with students doing their best to interrupt speakers...*[51]

Speakers from both sides of the political aisle have raised the ire of the politically correct who want to make sure that no one is offended—except, of course, the speakers, the people who want to hear them, and all those who value free speech.

Speakers and professors aren't the only victims of the PC movement. The CEO of tech company Mozilla was pushed out when the PC platoons launched a Twitter attack on him because he had given money to support a ban on gay marriage in California.[52] And Google fired a software engineer who sent out a memo "stating that women are biologically unsuited for engineering and other tech industry jobs."[53] That is definitely an obnoxious point of view. Had I been working at Google at the time, I would have found him and given a piece of my (woman's) mind. But did he deserve to lose his job because he voiced an opinion? And what was the stated cause? According to the engineer, he was terminated for the PC crime of "perpetuating gender stereotypes."

---

[51] "College students support free speech – unless it offends them." By Jeffrey J. Selingo. *Washington Post*, March 11, 2018. Viewed February 3, 2020. Accessible at https://www.washingtonpost.com/local/college-students-support-free-speech--unless-it-offends-them/2018/03/09/79f21c9e-23e4-11e8-94da-ebf9d112159c_story.html.

[52] "Mozilla CEO resignation raises free-speech issues." By AP. *USA Today*, April 4, 2014. Viewed February 3, 2020. Accessible at https://www.usatoday.com/story/news/nation/2014/04/04/mozilla-ceo-resignation-free-speech/7328759/.

[53] "Google's fired 'politically incorrect' engineer has sparked a broad ideological debate." By Aja Romano. *Vox*, August 9, 2017. Viewed February 3, 2020. Accessible at https://www.vox.com/culture/2017/8/9/16112050/google-fired-engineer-james-damore-alt-right-free-speech.

Even newspapers, whose freedom of the press has been protected by the First Amendment for almost 230 years, may punish those who say the "wrong" thing. Joe Caldara, a columnist for the *Denver Post*, lost his job for asserting that sex is binary; that a person is either male or female. The *Denver Post*, by the way, prides itself on "having a wide variety of voices in our pages" and says it is "looking for both conservative and liberal writers." That is, it wants these writers as long as they don't say that men are men and women are women.[54] The *Denver Post*'s official reason for firing Caldara was because it does not want to "run conservative columns about issues surrounding sex and gender…"[55]

Professors, executives, writers, speakers—no matter who we are or what we do, we're all subject to the wrath of the PC promoters. And we're all at risk of verbal and physical attack and losing our livelihood, reputation, and peace of mind.

The PC Follies

Actually, most of us are not going to lose our jobs or be physically threatened in the name of political correctness because we've been cowed into submission. We've learned to think carefully about everything we do and say, then muzzle ourselves, just as people did in communist Czechoslovakia. For example, we've learned *not* to say things like:

---

[54] "Columnist Fired for Stating Sex is Binary." By Madeleine Kearns. *National Review*, January 22, 2020. Viewed February 3, 2020. Accessible at https://www.nationalreview.com/2020/01/transgender-politics-columnist-fired-for-stating-sex-is-binary/.

[55] "Social Liberal Is Silenced Over Belief That There Are 'Only 2 Sexes.'" By Nicole Russell. *Daily Signal*, January 23, 2020. Viewed February 3, 2020. Accessible at https://www.dailysignal.com/2020/01/23/jon-caldara-accuses-denver-post-of-silencing-him-over-sex-views/.

- "I want to die," because we might offend the suicidal.
- "basket case," because that was a description applied to World War I soldiers who lost both arms and both legs in battle and needed to be carried around in a basket (a litter).
- "long time no see," because this might offend people struggling to learn English, who could feel you are making fun of their syntax.
- "grandfathered in" because this phrase, which originated shortly after the Civil War, was used to describe a way to keep newly-freed blacks from voting. This apparently makes it offensive to millions of people who, until now, probably didn't know they were offended.

Of course, if you investigate the old meanings of words we use every day, you'll find that we are all constantly guilty of microaggression, macroaggression, and every aggression in between. "Goodbye," for example, comes from the phrase "God be with you." So saying goodbye to an atheist seems like a terrible insult to their beliefs. And how about the word "sinister," which comes from the Latin word for "left?" The Ancient Romans thought anyone who used his left hand was somehow evil. So aren't we insulting lefties every time we use this word?

Then there's the phrase "rule of thumb," which PCers consider sexist and vile because, so we've been told, it comes from an old law that allowed men to use a stick as wide as their thumbs to beat their wives. Oh, wait a minute, it turns out that the phrase actually originally meant "a roughly practical method."[56] Well, if we can't be offended over the original

---

[56] "On Language; Misrule of Thumb." By William Safire. *New York Times Magazine,* January 25, 1998. Viewed February 7, 2020. Accessible at https://www.nytimes.com/1998/01/25/magazine/on-language-misrule-of-thumb.html.

meaning it never had, PC folks can still get hopping mad over the meaning they *thought* it had. The PC follies go on and on.

Many of us have been cowed into accepting PC nonsense even when it's pushed to bizarre extremes. In 2017, in Seattle, Washington,[57] for example, the blocks surrounding King County Superior Court had become unsanitary (with sidewalks reeking of urine and excrement) and unsafe (with two jurors and half a dozen employees having been assaulted). Two King County Superior Court judges requested that the county "clean up the courthouse with a daily power-wash of the surrounding sidewalks..."

But council member Larry Gossett objected, saying, "he didn't like the idea of power-washing the sidewalks because it brought back images of the use of hoses against civil-rights activists."[58] Mr. Gossett didn't suggest a different solution to the problem. But maybe he thought it would be less offensive if workers were sent out to clean the sidewalks with shovels and pails, or perhaps toothbrushes—or would that be offensive to people with gum disease? Luckily, the city did not bow to this bit of PC insanity.

And how about the students from the University of California, Berkeley, who "demanded that they be excused from an in-class exam in their labor-issues class because they aren't privileged enough to be able to handle it emotionally...."[59]

---

[57] "From 2017: Judges complain it's unsafe, unsanitary outside King County Courthouse in Seattle." By Christine Clarridge. *Seattle Times*, originally published July 11, 2017. Viewed February 3, 2020. Accessible at https://www.seattletimes.com/seattle-news/crime/judges-complain-its-unsafe-unsanitary-outside-county-courthouse-in-seattle/.

[58] "Seattle-Area Councilman: Hosing Poop-Covered Sidewalks Might Be Racially Insensitive." By Katherine Timpf. *National Review*, July 12, 2017. Viewed February 3, 2020. Accessible at https://www.nationalreview.com/2017/07/city-councilman-hosing-poop-covered-sidewalks-might-be-racially-insensitive/.

[59] "Berkeley Students Insist They Cannot Take Their In-Class Exam Due to Lack of Privilege." By Katherine Timpf. *National Review*, October 5, 2017. Viewed

"Privilege" is the argument that white people set up this country, and all its schools, businesses, and everything else, in a way that favors whites and suppresses all others. As a result, only whites have the "privilege" that lets them succeed in this country. These same students suggested that their professor was not qualified to teach their course because he was white. What could you possibly say to convince people who believe this country is so horrible, their only recourse, the only way they could possibly survive, is to take their college exams at home?

Fortunately, as with the sidewalk hosing, sanity prevailed, and the students were required to take the exam in the classroom, like the other students. But despite a few setbacks like these, PC marches bravely on!

Changing the Way We Think (So No One Feels Bad)

Our desire to avoid offending others may be good to a certain extent, but it often goes off the deep end. My two daughters are enthusiastic soccer players, determined to score the most goals in every game. Their school team is good and almost always wins. But recently, some of the parents from other teams complained that their kids weren't winning enough. They berated our coach and insisted that our team stop playing so well, or at least let our "B-squad" take over the field.

This is political correctness run amuck, and it sounds a whole lot like socialism to me. Everybody needs to be exactly the same, and no one is allowed to be better than anyone else. If there are inequities, we simply change things to ensure equality.

February 3, 2020. Accessible at https://www.nationalreview.com/2017/10/berkeley-students-exam-triggering-oppressive-students-color/.

Effort is not rewarded. The desire to excel is somehow bad, so we all strive to be mediocre. These ideas are dressed up as ways for us to care for others and make sure no one is hurt. In truth, they drastically erode our rights to be free individuals.

Here's another example. In Connecticut and other states, boys who identify as girls are allowed to compete on girl's high school sports teams. Some of these boys have won top ribbons in track and field at state finals.

Is this fair? I'll go way out on a PC limb here and say that males and females are not the same. Males are typically larger, have bigger muscles, and have more testosterone than females. Thus, teenage boys who compete with teenage girls in track and field, and certain other sports, have a decided advantage. Call me a Neanderthal throwback, but that's what I believe. And so do millions of other Americans. But what we believe is ignored in favor of what the boys believe, which is that they are girls. In fact, we're told that what we believe is flat out wrong and hurtful. According to Erin Buzuvis, Director of the Center of Gender and Sexuality Studies at Western New England College:

> *If you start to put limitations or exclusions on their participation... you are disregarding and disrespecting a population of students based on a core aspect of their identity...*[60]

Isn't it just as disrespectful to the girls to insist they compete with boys who have an obvious advantage because of their muscles and hormones?

---

[60] "Connecticut parents petition to bar transgender track athletes." By Cam Smith. *USA Today High School Sports*, June 6, 2018. Viewed February 4, 2020. Accessible at https://usatodayhss.com/2018/connecticut-parents-ban-transgender-track-athletes.

PC won't be satisfied until it has us all believing that boys are girls and girls are boys, excelling and winning is wrong, having to take your exams in class means suffering under "white privilege," trying to keep the sidewalks free of human feces is racist, saying "America is a melting pot" means you're a white racist, free speech is bad, and First Amendment should be rewritten to make sure no American is ever offended.

No Free Speech, No Freedom

Because I spent my first nineteen years living under communism, I know what it means to fight to hold on to my own thoughts and beliefs, amid constant brainwashing.

I know what it's like to have my language "cleansed," my words and actions scrutinized for any deviance from what's considered acceptable.

I saw what happened when people were afraid to speak their minds.

I saw how my parents' generation had been cowed, and how that ever-present, pervasive fear could make people shut down their souls.

I experienced firsthand the communist enforcement of political correctness—that is, the correct way to act as defined by those in power.

Political correctness is perhaps the most obvious form of creeping socialism in America. It begins as the changing of our language by "enlightened" people who probably really do want to help the disadvantaged and level the playing field. But it quickly progresses into brainwashing carried out by "thought police" who tell us what to think, believe, and say.

How far are we from the passing of legislation that does the same terrible thing?

Chapter Nine

I Feel So Bad!

At the beginning of the 1940s, when it seemed likely that the United States would go to war with Japan in the near future, the U.S. government worried about the loyalty of more than 100,000 people of Japanese ancestry living on the West Coast. If the Japanese Army invaded California, Oregon, or Washington State, would they assist the invaders as saboteurs or spies? The State Department assigned a man named Curtis Munson to find out.

Munson traveled up and down the West Coast, speaking to city and FBI officials, as well as intelligence officers from the Army and Marines. This was a very reasonable thing to do in the face of a potential threat: assess the situation and come to a rational conclusion *before* a problem arises. Munson then wrote his report, stating that "Japanese Americans are loyal and would pose little threat…."[61] His report was sent to the State Department, and copies were given to President Roosevelt, the Secretary of State, Attorney General, and other officials. In addition, FBI Director J. Edgar Hoover stated that there was no need to worry about the loyalty of the Japanese on the West Coast.

Then, in December 1941, Japan launched a vicious sneak attack on our naval base in Pearl Harbor, Hawaii. Over two thousand American servicemen were killed, and the U.S.

---

[61] "The Munson Report." *Digital History.* Viewed February 13, 2020. Accessible at http://www.digitalhistory.uh.edu/active_learning/explorations/japanese_internment/munson_report.cfm.

Pacific Fleet was severely damaged. Panic swept the nation, with people terrified that a Japanese invasion might occur at any moment, perhaps in Los Angeles or San Francisco. Suddenly, anyone of Japanese descent who was living on the West Coast was suspected of being a spy or saboteur for the evil Japanese empire.

And all at once, in spite of the findings of the Munson Report, despite J. Edgar Hoover, more than 100,000 Japanese and Japanese-Americans were swept out their homes and banished to internment camps, where they would be held for the next several years.

Top American officials knew there was no serious threat, but took action based on feelings rather than reason. The country was frightened, and the only way to stop the bad feelings was to round up all of those who triggered these feelings. So we did. And that's what we continue to do—act on feelings rather than reason—when we feel bad.

Feeling Bad About Guns

Feeling, not reason, recently spurred Representative Jennifer Wexton of Virginia to introduce the "Gun Violence Prevention Through Financial Intelligence Act" in Congress. Ms. Wexton wants to create a new federal law requiring banks and credit card companies to hand over information about certain purchases of firearms. As she explained, "Banks, credit card companies, and retailers have unique insight into the behavior and purchasing patterns that can help identify and prevent mass shootings..."[62]

---

[62] "Should Banks Be in the Gun Control Business?" By Noah Shepardson. *Reason*, February, 2020. Viewed February 13, 2020. Accessible at https://reason.com/2020/01/20/should-banks-be-in-the-gun-control-business/.

Ms. Wexton believes we can somehow divine who is likely to commit a mass shooting by sifting through credit card receipts to see who's buying a lot of guns. While it's true that some who commit these atrocities legally purchase a lot of weapons right before their sprees, many do not. The killer behind the 2012 Sandy Hook Elementary School massacre, for example, used guns belonging to his mother.

This is a case of feelings crushing reason. Naturally, we feel terrible about mass shootings. But in response, we act impulsively and irrationally. Ms. Wexton's act ignores the 4th amendment to the U.S. Constitution, which protects us against "unreasonable searches and seizures," including those involving our personal financial information. It also turns the presumption of innocence on its head by treating people as if they were guilty until proven innocent.

Not only is it blatantly unconstitutional, it's also impractical. Passing this act would lead to a lot of perfectly innocent people coming under suspicion, being hauled in for questioning, and maybe having their lawfully-purchased, registered guns being seized. It would also cause a deluge of accusations of racial or other types of profiling, for members of certain groups would invariably feel they were being targeted for investigation more often than other groups. And once banks and credit card companies began routinely handing over information about gun purchases to the feds, the bad guys would switch to cash. Only innocent people would continue using credit cards.

How about turning to reason, instead? We could take steps to identify and treat the mental illnesses that drive people to engage in these senseless shootings. We could stop glorifying mass murders, stop running endless stories in the media that may encourage copycats. We could allow people to carry weapons for defensive purposes if they have been trained and certified. We could eliminate gun-free zones, areas such as schools in which firearms are prohibited by federal law (excepting teachers and others specifically allowed to carry guns according to state law). As John Lott and Congressperson Thomas Massie pointed out in 2018:

> *Since 1950, all but six mass public shootings in America have occurred where citizens are banned from carrying guns. In Europe, which has suffered three of the four worst K-12 school shootings in history, every single mass public shooting has occurred in a gun-free zone. Unsurprisingly, killers try to avoid armed resistance.*[63]

All the gun laws might be tolerable if they worked. But as a 2018 RAND study found, "there is a shortage of evidence about the effects of most gun laws..." In other words, no one has been able to prove that gun-free zones or other laws restricting guns work, which means these laws are not based on science or reason. The same RAND study interviewed 95 experts on gun policy. These experts ranged across the ideological spectrum, from strongly pro-gun law to strongly anti-gun law, yet displayed "comparatively strong agreement" that the following steps would be helpful:

- strengthening the prohibition against people with mental health issues from having guns;

---

[63] "Gun-free school zones will not protect kids: A painful but honest lesson after last week's school shooting in Kentucky." By John R. Lott, Jr. and Thomas Massie. *NY Daily News*, January 29, 2018. Viewed March 21, 2020. Accessible at https://www.nydailynews.com/opinion/gun-free-school-zones-not-protect-kids-article-1.3786452.

- strengthening the requirement that lost or stolen guns be reported to the police;
- requiring felons and others forbidden from owning guns to turn them in;
- stepping up media campaigns designed to encourage parents to keep guns out of the hands of their children.

This is what the experts agree on, so if we want to do anything, it should be this. But unfortunately, when we feel bad, we want to do something "big" right now, like banning all guns. And in our rush to "solve the problem," we often ignore the fact that we're tossing a piece of our liberty to the government like it was a hot potato. Doing so may make us feel better now. But if we surrender a piece of our liberty every time we feel bad, sooner or later, we'll be out of liberty to give up, and that won't feel so good.

Many people don't keep the larger picture in mind. Instead, they focus on the bad feelings of the moment. That explains Representative Jillian Gilchrest's quest to put a 50 percent sales tax on ammunition.[64] Gilchrest, a member of the Connecticut State House of Representatives, feels so bad about gun violence that she completely ignores some very salient facts with her sales tax proposal, including:

- Making ammo more expensive doesn't mean everyone will stop buying it. If you think about it, a crazed person who intends to shoot people, and then maybe kill himself, probably won't worry too much about a credit card bill he can't pay next month.

[64] "Shoot down a 50 percent tax increase on ammunition." By Nicole Russell. *Washington Examiner*, February 7, 2019. Viewed February 14, 2020. Accessible at https://www.washingtonexaminer.com/opinion/shoot-down-a-50-percent-tax-increase-on-ammunition.

- Owning more ammunition—or guns—does not make a person more likely to commit violent crime. Israel and Switzerland, both of which have high rates of gun ownership or possession, have significantly lower rates of violent crime than do many European countries that strictly control guns.
- Most gun crime is committed using illegal firearms, which would be unaffected by Gilchrest's tax.
- There is no clear-cut relationship between violent crime or homicide rates and gun control legislation.[65]
- Violent crime has been dropping in the U.S. for decades.

I know what it's like to feel terror, dread, and grief because of gun violence. I live just an hour's drive away from Sandy Hook Elementary School, and the massacre that occurred there in 2012 was a 9/11 moment for me. My daughters were almost three years old at the time and with my in-laws, spending their first day ever away from me. I remember a horrible feeling churning in my gut when I heard the news. When my daughters finally got home that day, I couldn't stop hugging them.

But never once did I think it would be a good idea to raise the tax on ammo, or turn credit card companies into snoops, or ban AR-15 rifles. Yes, an AR-15 was used at Sandy Hook. People feel bad and want to ban those guns. Does that really make sense? Suppose a knife or baseball bat or hammer is used to kill people, should we ban all knives and bats and hammers? What about cars? They're used as weapons and in other criminal ways, such as carrying violent jerks to and from crime scenes, transporting illegal substances, and more.

---

[65] "Here are 8 Stubborn Facts on Gun Violence in America." By John Malcolm and Amy Swearer. Heritage Foundation, March 14, 2018. Viewed February 14, 2020. Accessible at https://www.heritage.org/crime-and-justice/commentary/here-are-8-stubborn-facts-gun-violence-america.

Banning weapons does nothing to change the criminal mindset; it only criminalizes items most often used for lawful purposes like hunting and self-defense. Our focus should be on identifying and treating those with mental health issues, prosecuting and confining criminals, and improving security.

I don't have strong personal feelings about guns. I enjoyed sport shooting when I was a teenager, but if I never touch another gun in my life, that's fine with me. What's not fine is being forced to surrender or even decrease my 2nd Amendment rights. I know from living under communism that the first thing oppressive governments do is disarm their citizens; take away their right of self-protection. This allows the government to grow larger and more oppressive, and less likely to be challenged. The slow erosion of our 2nd Amendment rights, through taxation, monitoring, and increased legislation, is a worrisome sign of governmental bullying. And like all bullies, the government won't be satisfied until it takes over completely.

While we're talking about jerks with weapons, how about the people who are currently ignoring orders to isolate themselves due to the COVID-19 coronavirus? One such coronavirus patient, a New Hampshire man, crossed state lines to attend a Dartmouth Business School event in Vermont, "despite having been directed to self-isolate."[66] Another man who attended the event now has the virus, and it's quite possible the first guy gave it to him. The virus is potentially fatal, and one person can spread it to scores of others—in a reported case, a single

[66] "New Hampshire Coronavirus Patients Breaks Quarantine to Attend Dartmouth Event." By Melissa Godin. *Time*, March 4, 2020. Viewed March 21, 2020. Accessible at https://time.com/5795405/new-hampshire-coronavirus-patient-breaks-quarantine-to-attend-dartmouth-event/?utm_source=facebook&utm_medium=social&utm_campaign=editorial&utm_term=u.s._&linkId=83620276.

man in New York passed it on to fifty others.[67] So who is more dangerous? The one who deliberately spews potentially fatal germs at others, or the one who owns guns for sport or self-protection? And looking back across the decades, what of those who knew they had AIDS but did not take proper precautions when having sex? That certainly helped spread the disease and kill people. I wonder how many people have been "murdered by germ." Enforcing quarantine laws may be much more effective than the gun laws, which are absolutely *not* supported by science and reason.

Feeling Bad About Lobbyists

Senator Elizabeth Warren of Massachusetts has come up with a balm for her unhappy feelings: tax the corporate lobbyists. She wants to slap a 35 percent tax on lobbying expenditures between one-half and one million dollars, a 60 percent tax on those over $1 million, and a 75 percent tax on those above $5 million.[68] This would be over and above the income and business taxes lobbyists already pay.

Many people support this idea because lobbyists are not terribly popular. And since we're facing a huge federal budget deficit, it might seem like a good idea to raise some extra money while simultaneously making it harder for lobbyists to push their agendas.

---

[67] "New York officials traced more than 50 coronavirus cases back to one attorney." By Sheena Jones and Christina Maxouris. *CNN*, updated March 11, 2020. Viewed March 21, 2020. Accessible at https://www.cnn.com/2020/03/11/us/new-rochelle-attorney-containment-area/index.html.

[68] "Elizabeth Warren Wants To Tax Lobbying." By Peter Suderman. *Reason*, January, 2020. Viewed February 13, 2020. Accessible at https://reason.com/2019/12/19/elizabeth-warren-wants-to-tax-lobbying/.

Ah, but which lobbyists do we want to put a lid on? There are all kinds of lobbyists bending lawmakers' ears, not just those representing "evil" corporations or other groups you disapprove of. You may not like *those* lobbyists. But if you're past middle age, you may like AARP's lobbyists. If you're a fan of Florida football, you may be happy there are lobbyists for the Tampa Bay Buccaneers. There are also lobbyists for the Humane Society of the U.S., Sloan-Kettering Cancer Center, the Motion Picture Association, the Cannabis Trade Federation, Christian Care Ministry, McDonald's, Pinterest, and Yelp. Lots of companies and causes hire lobbyists, and many of them are working on your side. In truth, we *have* to hire lobbyists to represent us in Washington D.C., the many state capitals and numerous city halls, because our government is so big. Lobbying is one of the few (if not the only) way that groups or companies can make their voices heard.

I'm not in love with this situation. I'd rather be able to text my congressperson and arrange a 15-minute sit-down so we can talk about water zoning laws and gun-free zones. But that's not how it works. Government is too big. So we hire people to represent our interests.

Yes, we feel bad about lobbyists, and it may feel good to tax them. But taxing them only makes it more expensive to lobby. That won't hurt the big corporations because they have plenty of money. It will only hurt the smaller groups, some of which won't be able to afford representation in D.C. anymore. And how will that help you when you need to find a way for your voice to be heard?

"We can end excessive lobbying," Senator Warren has tweeted.[69]

69

I have a better idea: let's end excessive government. And if we need to tax something to feel better, let's tax government.

Feeling Bad About So Many Things

When we're feeling bad, it's so much easier to respond emotionally rather than turn to reason. Consider these examples:

- Certain Democrats in Connecticut, upset about the spread of "extreme right views," have proposed a new state law that would "finance and create a new department at the Connecticut State Police which will specialize in investigating far-right extremist groups and individuals."[70] Note that this is an *entirely new* force specifically created to go after far-right extremists. Not all extremists, or leftist extremists, or homegrown communists, only those on the "far right." Going after people on the right may make some people feel better, and improve a politician's vote count in a heavily Democratic state, but it's discrimination, plain and simple. And, the last I checked, holding certain political views are not legal offenses. Sounds exactly like communism, to me.
- A group of Republicans in the Tennessee House of Representatives feels bad that President Trump has been severely criticized by many media outlets. In response, they have introduced a bill "that would recognize CNN and the Washington Post 'as fake news' that is 'part

[70] "Looney, Duff, State Democrats Announce 'A Just Connecticut' Agenda." A press release from the office of Senate President Pro Tempore Martin M. Looney. January 22, 2020. Viewed February 14, 2020. Accessible at http://www.senatedems.ct.gov/looney-news/3045-looney-200122#sthash.xHba9oNB.uTLXzf85.dpbs.

of the media wing of the Democratic party.'"[71] This is nothing if not a blatant attack on the free press, an attempt to undermine the first amendment. It may feel good to some, but the free press is an essential element of our freedom, even when we don't like what the "other side" may be saying.

- Former congressman Beto O'Rourke of Texas feels bad because certain religious institutions (churches, schools, and charities) are opposed to same-sex marriage. His response is to try to strip them of the tax-except status granted to all religious institutions. O'Rourke admitted he was "throwing all political or polling caution to the wind" in proposing this.[72] And that's not all; he's also throwing religious freedom to the wind. He wants the federal government to decide which religious organizations are "good" and which are "bad." This takes us perilously close to erasing the first amendment admonition against setting up a favorite religion for the nation. You may or may not like same-sex marriage. But when you start using taxes as a way to keep religions in line, you've crossed the Rubicon.
- The State of California feels bad about bullying and body-shaming. Thus, the state government has decided that asking students to state whether they identify as either male or female, as part of the standard physical

[71] "Tennessee Republican bids to classify CNN and the Washington Post as 'fake news.'" By Kenya Evelyn. *The Guardian*, February 12, 2020. Viewed February 14, 2020. Accessible at https://www.theguardian.com/us-news/2020/feb/12/tennessee-republican-cnn-washington-post-fake-news?CMP=Share_AndroidApp_Gmail.

[72] "Beto O'Rourke said he would revoke tax-except status from religious organizations that oppose same-sex marriage." By Jeffery Cook. *ABC News*, October 11, 2019. Viewed February 14, 2020. Accessible at https://abcnews.go.com/Politics/beto-orourke-revoke-tax-exempt-status-religious-organizations/story?id=66213718.

fitness tests, is discriminatory to those who identify as neither, and that it leads to bullying and body-shaming. But instead of clamping down on those doing the bullying and body-shaming, California has suspended the tests.[73] So now, a tiny percentage of students won't have to feel bad about saying whether they are a girl or a boy. Meanwhile, all students will continue to feel the wrath of bullies, who will instantly find other targets. And soon enough, the entire state will suffer as the population becomes less physically fit, more obese, and more likely to develop diabetes and other diseases.

- California must be very alert to the slightest slight because officials at that state's Santa Clara University posted a dire warning for their students on their "Bias Incident Reporting" webpage. Students were instructed to "ALWAYS CALL 911 IMMEDIATELY" when bias occurred.[74] (Yes, the instructions were in all capital letters, and bolded, too!) This means that students who feel bad because they think someone has slighted them because of "actual or perceived race, color, national origin, ethnicity, religious affiliation, sex, gender identity, disability, or sexual orientation," should call 911 immediately. Don't worry about clogging up the phone lines normally reserved for reporting things like car crashes, heart attacks, and muggings in progress.

[73] "California may stop school fitness tests over fears they lead to bullying and body-shaming." By Alicia Lee. *CNN*, February 6, 2020. Viewed February 17, 2020. Accessible at https://www.cnn.com/2020/02/06/us/california-fitness-test-bullying-trnd/index.html.

[74] The university's webpage has since been change, but you can see the original on WebArcihve.org. See "Bias Incident Reporting," Santa Clara University. Viewed February 17, 2020. Accessible at http://web.archive.org/web/20150611154725/http:/www.scu.edu/provost/diversity/education_training/biasincidentreporting.cfm.

Forget about that nonsense. Get right on with 911 and let them know you're feeling really bad!

- The student government at the University of Minnesota-Twin Cities rejected a resolution to have a "moment of recognition" during anniversaries of the 9/11 terrorist attacks. Why? Because Muslim students might feel offended. And if that wasn't offensive enough, David Algadi, the university's Director of Diversity and Inclusion, asked, "When will we start having moments of silence for all of the times white folks have done something terrible?"[75] Apparently, it's not okay to honor the victims of the 9/11 attacks because that might offend Muslims. But it's fine to make white folks feel bad by making remarks like this one. How is that inclusive?
- The all-female Mount Holyoke College in South Hadley, Massachusetts canceled a production of the well-known play called "The Vagina Monologues." Why? Not because the mention of the vagina is considered offensive, but because not all people who identify as women have vaginas.[76] In other words, the play was "blatantly transphobic."[77] It would make men-who-became-women feel bad because they lacked a vagina,

[75] "MSA Rejects Moment of Recognition Resolution for 9/11." Author Removed. *Minnesota Republic*, November 11, 2015. Viewed February 17, 2020. Accessible at https://mnrepublic.com/2620/uncategorized/msa-rejects-moment-of-recognition-resolution-for-911/.

[76] "Women's College Cancels 'Vagina Monologues' Because It Excludes Women Without Vaginas." By Elizabeth Nolan Brown. *Reason*, January 1, 2015. Viewed February 17, 2020. Accessible at https://reason.com/2015/01/15/womens-college-cancels-vagina-monologues/.

[77] "Women's College Cancels 'Vagina Monologues' Because It Excludes Women Without Vaginas." By Elizabeth Nolan Brown. *Reason*, January 1, 2015. Viewed February 17, 2020. Accessible at https://reason.com/2015/01/15/womens-college-cancels-vagina-monologues/.

and maybe make women-who-became-men feel bad because they still had one.

- In my hometown of Glastonbury, two boys who identify as girls were permitted to join the girl's track team. Not surprisingly, within the past three years, they have won fifteen state championships between them. Equally unsurprisingly, three girl track runners have sued the state. They argue that allowing boys who identify as girls to compete as girls discriminates against girls who actually are girls and that forcing girls to compete against boys in a girl's sport makes it nearly impossible for them to succeed. So, because the trans girls felt bad about being boys, they've hijacked the girl's sport. Now the girls have been forced to go to court to reclaim their rights and possibly their opportunities to win college scholarships.

Feeling Bad is No Reason to Pass a Law

Every time something bad happens, people demand that the government do something. "There ought to be a law!" No, there *shouldn't* be a new law passed every time we feel bad.

First of all, rushing to pass new laws is never a good idea. They may make us feel better at the moment, but such laws rarely solve the underlying problem. They're usually just Band-Aids that let the infection fester beneath. Secondly, they make the government bigger, diminishing our individual rights while making us weaker and more dependent.

We already have way too many laws, many of which aren't being enforced. For instance, a study looked at recently-passed laws in Colorado, Delaware, and Washington State requiring comprehensive background checks of people who wanted to buy guns. The researchers found that only one of the three states (Delaware) actually had an increase in background checks.[78] It's not clear why. Maybe the other states didn't devote enough resources to enforcing the laws, or maybe the citizens refused to comply. Obviously, just passing a law when we feel bad doesn't necessarily solve the problem.

In fact, in most cases, rushing to write new laws when tragedy strikes is just pretending to do something.

If we really want to make a difference, we must push beyond our feelings. That's because feelings scream for us to fork over our power to the "big daddy" who can make things better, now! Reason, on the other hand, tells us that there are usually deeper-rooted problems that must be addressed, and that giving away our power is not the answer. Not in the long run.

The government is *not* the answer to every problem we have. It is not our nanny. Neither is it our moral compass. It is supposed to protect and preserve the republic, and protect and preserve our rights—period.

When we involve the government in our everyday affairs, we pay for it by losing our God-given freedoms. That's why more legislation is rarely a satisfactory solution to our problems.

---

[78] Castillo-Carnigila A, Kagawa RMC, Webster DW, et al. "Comprehensive background check policy and background checks in three US states." *Inj Prev*. 2018 Dec;24(6):431-436. doi: 10.1136/injuryprev-2017-042475. Epub 2017 Oct 6. Viewed February 18, 2020. Accessible at https://www.ncbi.nlm.nih.gov/pubmed/28986427.

Chapter Ten

No Safe Spaces at 5,000 Feet

I have a very clear memory of my first parachute jump. I wanted to jump to impress my father, who was an avid skydiver. So at age fifteen, I eagerly raced through the training, which was offered to "approved" youngsters to prepare them for military service, learning things like how to roll when landing so I wouldn't break my legs, and how to pack my chute. This last bit involved gathering the chute after landing, folding it perfectly, and stuffing it back into the casing in a very particular way. This had to be done exactly right, or it wouldn't open properly on the next jump—which meant it could very well be my last.

I sat quietly in an old Soviet cargo plane with about twenty other jumpers, plus my father, who was our instructor, for about a quarter of an hour as it climbed to 5,000 feet. Then, when my father gave the command, we all stood up, grabbed our cords, and hooked them to the static line, which ran from the front of the plane to the back. First-time jumpers like me used the static line to make sure our chutes opened automatically after jumping. There was always the danger that a novice might open it too soon or too late, or panic and not open it all.

I remember the roar of the plane's engines and the power of the wind, once the plane's door was thrown open. I stood in line, slowly moving forward, watching those ahead of me jump out of the plane, one at a time. Surprisingly, I felt okay; not too nervous. My father stood at the door, shouting final instructions and words of encouragement to the nervous nellies in front of me as they approached. When it was finally my turn to stand at the door, I suddenly had a stomach full of butterflies, and wasn't the least bit eager to take the leap. I guess I hesitated a little too long because the next thing I knew, a hand slammed into my back, propelling me through the door and out into the wild blue yonder. I managed to turn my head quickly enough to catch a glimpse of my father's face. And as I fell backward toward the earth, all I could think was, "DAD!!!!"

It must have been a funny sight, my face flattened by the wind, and my body sprawled and awkward as I fell through the air at 120 miles an hour. I was terrified by the sound of the wind screaming in my ears, until my chute opened abruptly, and all went quiet. Just like that, everything became peaceful, even beautiful, as I drifted toward earth. All too soon, the ground was rushing toward me, so I assumed the landing position, hit the ground with a roll, and jumped right up.

I loved it!

I would go on to make many jumps and, although each one was an indescribable thrill, it also had the potential to end my life. Every year at least a couple of jumpers died due to faulty parachutes, collisions with the plane or other jumpers, or other problems. The undeniable truth is there are no safe spaces at 5,000 feet. That's the main reason most people wouldn't skydive. It's just too risky.

Skydiving might not have scared me as much as it frightened others because I was used to being unsafe. There were no safe spaces anywhere in Czechoslovakia; or in any other socialist or communist countries, for that matter. Fearful and cruel, our leaders clamped down hard on us if we dared to challenge them. Political arguments simply weren't allowed. Those who crossed our leaders might be taken to the police station for a "talking to" or put in jail. They could lose their jobs or apartments, or they might even be killed.

There was nothing we could do about this but rebel, which Czechoslovakia tried and failed to do in 1968. Otherwise, we just had to wait until communism collapsed. And, in the meantime, we had to put up with being unsafe.

I came to the U.S. because I wanted to escape an insecure, even dangerous future. And yet, today, I see that many Americans are pushing hard to make us unsafe, here in the land of liberty. Ironically, they're doing this by trying to create "safe spaces" for certain groups of people.

What Are "Safe Spaces?"

The idea of safe spaces dates back to the earliest human beings, who were seeking shelter from the weather, as well as protection from enemies and animals. Finding a safe space was often a matter of life and death, and banding together with others was vital. As time went on, it became necessary to form groups in order to build and govern communities, establish trade, set up cooperative ventures like farming and livestock raising, and allow some people to specialize, increasing the ability of the entire group to survive. Forming groups was also a good social activity, as people enjoyed the company of others in pubs, clubs, private homes, and other gathering spots. This coming together by choice usually worked well, especially in small, homogenous societies where differences between group members were relatively small. They were safe spaces where people could gather, solve problems, take care of each other, and enjoy life.

Today there's a different definition of a safe space. It began on college campuses, where various groups of students wanted a place where they could occasionally gather for discussions, support sessions, parties, or just hanging out. What's wrong with that? Well, initially, a safe space was a place where members of a particular group could gather to share experiences, support each other, and feel comfortable. But it has morphed into a way for these groups to exclude all others and any ideas they may find offensive. Safe-spacers were once content to have a room to themselves for an occasional evening; now they are demanding rooms and even entire dormitories that are devoted exclusively and permanently to them. It's segregation, pure and simple, done in the name of safety.

A 2019 report by the National Association of Scholars noted that the demand for safe spaces has required many colleges and universities to reintroduce segregation to American campuses:

> .... *in the new form of segregation (neo-segregation), colleges eagerly recruit black and other minority students, but actively foster campus arrangements that encourage these students to form separate social groups on campus.*[79]

Neo-segregation includes having separate student orientations, dormitories, graduation ceremonies, and more, according to race.

---

[79] "Neo-Segregation at Yale. A Report by the National Association of Scholars." By Dion J. Pierre and Peter W. Wood. National Association of Scholars, April, 2019. Viewed March 10, 2020. Accessible at https://www.nas.org/storage/app/media/Reports/NeoSeg%20at%20Yale/NeoSegregation_at_Yale.pdf. See also an article on the report written by Dion Pierre: "Demands for Segregated Housing at Williams College Are Not News." Dion J. Pierre. *National Review*, May 8, 2019. Viewed March 10, 2020. Accessible at https://www.nationalreview.com/2019/05/american-colleges-segregated-housing-graduation-ceremonies/.

The idea is that certain groups need places where they can feel safe, but the safe-space movement is actually pushing societal groups further apart. By walling themselves off and creating their own separate worlds, they are increasing the level of distrust, animosity, and tribalism among our diverse population. And in the process, they are making everyone less safe. They are reinforcing the feeling that "the other" is irredeemably evil and must be kept at arm's length, if not crushed. They are also making it seem that engaging with "the other" is more trouble than it's worth; it's easier and safer to stay on "our side" of the line. So people warily, sometimes angrily, back away from each other. This is the antithesis of what America, the great melting pot, is supposed to be.

We Need to Cross the Lines, Not Draw More of Them

In the late 1780s, the recently-formed United States was trying to decide whether or not to adopt what became our Constitution. The debate played out, in part, in newspaper articles, written by people who used pen names that harkened back to ancient Rome. These names were supposed to remind readers of certain revered principles of governance. In one such article, the author, "Brutus," stated that:

> *In a republic, the manners, sentiments, and interests of the people should be similar. If this be not the case, there will be a constant clashing of opinions; and the representatives of one part will be continually striving against those of the other. This will retard the operations of*

government, and prevent such conclusions as will promote the public good.[80]

Brutus was pointing out the obvious: In a republic, the people need to have strong similarities because they have to work together to determine their future. The more their opinions differ, and the more they fight against each other, the more difficult it will be to govern effectively. That makes perfect sense. And back when the United States began, it was possible to find plenty of common ground between the people involved since they tended to come from the same places and have similar desires.

Today, of course, it's not possible that some 330 million Americans will share the same "manners, sentiments, and interests." There are too many of us, and our backgrounds are too diverse. Although we value our diversity of ideas and opinions, religions and cuisines, historical and cultural reference points, and much more, we're also tribal by nature, wary of the stranger, and worried about our own positions in society. Yet Brutus' point about being similar and working together is as valid today as it was in the 1700s. That is why we must make every effort to reach across the lines of race and religion, language and culture, and other divisions, to come together as one, rather than as countless individual groups warily eyeing each other from our respective corners. That is why creating "safe spaces" for various groups is a bad idea. We need *fewer* boundaries between groups, not more. We need *more* mixing, even though it will create more friction between groups and individuals. Sooner or later that friction will wear down the edges between us, and in doing so, it will bring us closer together.

---

[80] From "Document 6: Brutus I." Found in **50 Core American Documents**. Edited by Christopher Burkett. Ashbrook Press, 2015. Chapter 6, "Brutus I." Pages 44-45.

Safety Gone Wrong

It's not just students making these safe-space demands, and it's not just about finding a "place of their own." College and university professors have gotten involved in "student safety," sometimes to a ridiculous degree. In March 2017, six professors from the prestigious Wellesley College announced their concern about the negative effect they believed certain speakers had on students. Many students, the professors asserted, were "in distress as a result of a speaker's words," and "often feel the injury most acutely, and invest time and energy in rebutting the speakers' arguments." Thus, although the professors insist that they "defend free speech and believe it is essential to a liberal art education," they offered themselves up as what would essentially be a censorship committee to decide who could speak on campus and who couldn't.[81] In short, they wanted to make the entire campus a safe space, protecting students from hearing the "wrong" speakers talking about the "wrong" things. Is it just me, or does that sound like something straight out of dictatorship?

Here's another one: Yale University's Intercultural Affairs Committee sent out an email in 2015 asking students not to wear "culturally unaware and insensitive" costumes that might distress minority students, including turbans and feathered headdresses. The Committee asserted that, even if students did not realize their costumes were offensive, "their actions or lack of forethought have sent a far greater message than any apology could after the fact..."[82] In other words, even a

---

[81] Email from Michael P. Jeffries to Faculty-Staff Discussion. Dated March 20, 2017. Viewed March 10, 2020. Accessible at https://www.thefire.org/subject-facstaffdiscuss-statement-cere-faculty-re-laura-kipnis-freedom-project-visit-aftermath/.

[82] "Email From the Intercultural Affairs Committee." *Fire*, October 27, 2015. Viewed March 10, 2020. Accessible at https://www.thefire.org/email-from-intercultural-affairs/.

foolish slip followed by an apology might cause horrible and irreparable damage.

Faculty member Erika Christakis protested, insisting that the students should wear any costumes they liked without worrying about offending others. If other students were offended, they should look away. This unleashed a flood of criticism and led to Ms. Christakis' resignation. Her husband, also a Yale faculty member, was confronted by a group of Yale students who demanded that he apologize for his wife's views, which he shared. When he refused to do so, they cursed and verbally abused him in a heated, face-to-face confrontation, viewable on YouTube.[83] (The exchange becomes alarming at the 30-second mark.)

Hoping to nip problems like these in the bud, in 2016, the Dean of Students at Tufts University encouraged "all students that feel like they have encountered someone who is wearing an inappropriate and offensive costume to please file a report..."[84] Complaints could result in disciplinary action and/or a police investigation.

There were no hard-and-fast guidelines, however, about which costumes might be considered offensive. Some may be obvious, like Nazi uniforms or get-ups requiring a black or red face. But is a samurai costume offensive to Japanese-Americans? Or is a World War II American Army uniform offensive to a Japanese-American whose grandparents spent

[83] Foundation for Individual Rights in Education. "Yale University Students Protest Halloween Costume Email." November 6, 2015. Video, 1:20. Viewed March 10, 2020. Accessible at https://www.youtube.com/watch?v=9IEFD JVYd0&feature=youtu.be.

[84] "Campus Costume Cops Ask Students to Report 'Inappropriate' Halloween Costumes." By Robby Soave. *Daily Beast*, updated April 13, 2017. Viewed March 10, 2020. Accessible at https://www.thedailybeast.com/campus-costume-cops-ask-students-to-report-inappropriate-halloween-costumes.

time in a relocation camp during the war? How about a Pocahontas costume?

This is insanity! Of all the places we pass through in life, the college campus is ideally suited to help us reach across lines. College campuses are supposed to expose young minds to different, challenging, and sometimes even insulting ideas. Away from the protective influence of parents, students can open their minds to new ideas and new experiences. They can interact with "the other" in the classroom and the dorms, at meals, and in social gatherings. They can learn how to argue vigorously with "the other" and even grow angry, yet still break bread together. They can get to know people from other groups as individuals and better understand their points of view. And yet, campuses are increasingly "protecting" students from these kinds of experiences in the name of being "sensitive."

Van Jones, formerly an advisor to President Barak Obama, had this to say about safe spaces and shielding students from distressing ideas:

> *I think that's a terrible idea for the following reason: I don't want you to be safe ideologically. I don't want you to be safe emotionally. I want you to be strong... You are creating a kind of liberalism that the minute it crosses the street into the real world is not just useless but obnoxious and dangerous.*[85]

Students need to leave their safe spaces. Or better yet, to never enter them in the first place.

---

[85] "Safe Spaces On College Campuses Are Creating Intolerable Students." By Flemming Rose. *HuffPost*, updated June 12, 2017. Viewed March 10, 2020. Accessible at https://www.huffpost.com/entry/safe-spaces-college-intolerant_b_58d957a6e4b02a2eaab66ccf.

Let's Engage!

We are a large nation made up of all races and religions, of people from all over the world. We will never all see eye to eye on everything. And this is a good thing, for our diversity introduces new ideas that can benefit us greatly—all of us. But we must constantly strive to break down barriers between each other, not build new ones. We must constantly look for ways to build bridges that connect us to each other, even if it means exposing ourselves to offensive outlooks. In fact, *especially* when it means doing so. Retreating from distressing ideas, opinions, and people is a *loss* of liberty.

You lose liberty when you only interact with others who share your thoughts, experiences, and background because you forget how to be with "the other." You become more convinced of the righteousness of your cause, and more and more suspicious of those with differing opinions. You lock yourself into a tiny world of your own making, which makes you *less* free, not more.

We need to leave our safe spaces, not create more of them. Yes, it can sometimes feel like jumping out of an airplane. And maybe someone might need to give us a little shove to get us to take the leap. But it's the only way you can truly fly.

Chapter Eleven

Ask Me Not, Give Me All

It was an iconic moment in American history. John Fitzgerald Kennedy, the charismatic young war hero who had won the 1960 presidential election, stood on the porch of the U.S. Capital Building, took the oath of office, and then, in his inaugural address, uttered the words which thrilled the nation: "And so, my fellow Americans: Ask *not* what your country can do for you—ask what *you* can do for your country."

These words swept across the nation, inspiring millions of Americans to pledge their lives to the service of their nation by becoming teachers, joining the brand-new Peace Corps, and otherwise look for ways to help their communities, their nation, and people around the world. Kennedy excited people with his can-do philosophy, captured so beautifully in his speech, saying that he does not shrink from responsibility, he welcomes it.

Less than three years later, he was assassinated, and Vice-President Lyndon Johnson took the helm. Like Kennedy, Johnson wanted to help people. But, in many ways, he turned Kennedy's ideas upside down when he launched his massive "War on Poverty." Much like Roosevelt's "New Deal" of the 1930s, Johnson's program called for a major expansion of the federal government, with new acts, offices, bureaucratic rules and regulations, taxes and expenditures. Government money would be lavished on education, community development, job training, and more. Social security and food stamp programs were beefed up, and Project Head Start offered early education, nutrition, and health services to low-income children. Medicaid was created to help poor people pay for health care, and much more was done to eradicate poverty.

President Johnson's heart was in the right place, but his head obviously wasn't because the program turned out to be a failure. He had wanted to give people a "hand up," not a "hand-out"—just enough assistance so they would be able to support themselves and their families, educate their children, and otherwise become self-sufficient. He insisted that the War on Poverty's massive outlay of money and services would get people *off* the welfare rolls, not on them. The result? Today, some 36 million Americans (about ten percent of the nation) rely on the Supplemental Nutrition and Assistance Program (SNAP) to help buy their food.[86] And this is just one of a plethora of federal and state programs offering assistance for food, education, housing and more—including the Special Supplemental Food Program for Women, Infants and Children (WIC), the Child Nutrition Program, subsidies for the Affordable Care Act, Medicaid, the Child's Health Insurance Program (CHIP), the Low-Income Home Energy Assistance Program (LIHEAP), Supplemental Security Income Program (SSI), and Head Start.

The sad truth is our society has developed a "hand-out" mentality. We've become increasingly dependent on the government as we clamor for grants and programs, designation as part of a "protected" or "disadvantaged" class, grants, tax exemptions, and other hand-outs. Far too many of us expect the federal, state, and local governments to take care of us, guide us through life, and make decisions, major and minor, for us. And there's no sign that this way of thinking will be reversed any time soon, if at all.

---

[86] "How Trump's New Food Stamp Rule Could Impact Nearly 700,000 Vulnerable Americans." By Jasmine Aguilera. *Time*, December 9, 2019. Viewed March 4, 2020. Accessible at https://time.com/5744647/trump-food-stamps-rule/.

Here are just two of the more ridiculous examples that illustrate how much we've come to rely on the government, how we go running to the government for help at the first sign of trouble.

In the first case, California's legislature is considering a law that would forbid large department stores from separating children's items by gender.[87] That is, it would be illegal to have one aisle for boys' clothing and one for girls', one area for girls' toys and one for boys', one place for childcare items for boys and another place for girls. Instead, all the clothing for children would have to be placed in the "kids' clothing" area, and the same for toys and childcare items. Stores that failed to comply would be hit with $1,000 fines.

As I write this, California is facing huge, ongoing problems with drought, its multi-billion-dollar bullet train boondoggle, homelessness, people being priced out of the housing markets in many cities, massive fires triggered by downed power lines every time the wind blows strongly, and school kids performing under par up and down the state. But this is what they're worried about?

Setting aside the fact that a fair number of people like having children's items separated by sex—I know I do when shopping for my daughters—do we really have to pass a law about this? And then have bureaucrats follow-up with rules and regulations, so inspectors know what to look for when ferreting out flaunters of the law? Suppose a store dutifully puts all the kids' toys in a single aisle but sets trucks on one shelf and

[87] The law would apply to department stores with over 500 employees. See "'Gender neutral' plan for toys would get rid of boys' and girls' aisles in California stores." By Andrew Sheeler. *Sacramento Bee*, February 26, 2020. Viewed March 4, 2020. Accessible at https://www.sacbee.com/news/politics-government/capitol-alert/article240601601.html?fbclid=IwAR17bMuR5UIC8r3MMpQ_x9CeUqUSHkYzozwDhBDrLG-5Vot8CM3bsPZ-dF4.

Barbie dolls on another? Is that a violation of the law? Who knows? We'll need hearings, expert testimony, and regulations about this!

Wouldn't it make more sense for people offended by the existence of "blue aisles" and "pink aisles" to write letters of protest to the stores, start a "No Pink, No Blue" group on Facebook, or organize a boycott? When our Founding Fathers were offended, they dumped British tea into Boston harbor. They organized a Continental Congress, wrote a Declaration of Independence, and went to war. What do we do today? We go running to the government to pass a law against separating boys' toys from girls' toys.

California is also worried about the "pink tax,"[88] caused by routinely higher prices for "women's items." There's no doubt that women pay more than men for razors, sportswear, soccer balls, and other items designed specifically for them. Like pink razors that are the same as the blue ones for men, but just a little smaller, or maybe have a thinner handle. A study conducted by the New York City Department of Consumer Affairs found that "on average… women's products cost 7 percent more than similar products for men.[89] That's because manufacturers have found that women will pay more for certain products if they're in pretty packaging and advertised with "feminine" slogans.

Because of this, the State of California is currently considering a law to end the "pink tax." This bill would "prohibit a business establishment from discriminating against a person

---

[88] "Axing the 'pink tax' + Consumer Watchdog sues Lara + California fights Trump school rules." By Hannah Wiley. *Sacramento Bee*. February 19, 2020. Viewed March 4, 2020. Accessible at https://www.sacbee.com/news/politics-government/capitol-alert/article240401766.html.

[89] "From Cradle to Cane: The Cost of Being a Female Consumer." New York City Department of Consumer Affairs, December, 2015. Viewed March 4, 2020. Accessible at https://www1.nyc.gov/site/dca/partners/gender-pricing-study.page.

because of a person's gender with respect to the price charged for any 2 consumer products from the same manufacturer that are substantially similar if those products are priced differently based on the gender of the individuals for whose use the products are intended or marketed, as specified."[90]

Naturally, California will have to hold hearings, write new regulations, send out inspectors armed with new "anti-pink tax forms," issue fines, and sue stores that don't comply. But suppose some manufacturer sets up separate "blue" and "pink" subsidiaries, using that as a dodge to get around the new law? Or hires clever lawyers to split hairs over the definition of "substantially similar?" What will happen then? We'll need more hearings, laws, and regulations, of course.

Here's a better idea: stop buying the stuff! If enough women "boycott pink" for a couple of weeks, prices will come tumbling down.

Running to the government every time problems arise weakens us by reinforcing the idea that we can't do anything on our own. At the same time, it strengthens government, in the wrong way, by giving it more power over commerce, more reason to tax us, and more influence over the decisions we can make in our daily lives. Many of us are doing less thinking and acting for ourselves, and looking more to the government for help. Instead of asking ourselves what *we* can do for our country, we're asking what our country can do for *us*.

Let's look at just a few of the things we're currently begging the government to handle for us: jobs, housing, and income.

---

[90] Senate Bill-873 Gender: discrimination: pricing. California Legislative Information. Viewed March 4, 2020. Accessible at http://leginfo.legislature.ca.gov/faces/billTextClient.xhtml?bill_id=201920200SB873.

Give Me a Job!

The federal government has long been a provider of jobs: soldiers, managers, janitors, clerical staff, engineers, mail delivery people, inspectors, researchers, and so on. Indeed, as of 2019, there were "2.1 million federal employees, 4.1 million contract employees, 1.2 million grant employees, 1.3 million active-duty military personnel, and more than 500,000 postal service employees."[91] All told, about six percent of those who work, work for Uncle Sam.

In recent years, some people have suggested the federal government be required to offer a job to anyone who wants one. Not anytime the government needs a new employee, but whenever someone wants work. Everyone would be guaranteed a job, no matter what their skill or education level, location, past work history, aptitude, or attitude toward work. Senator Bernie Sanders of Vermont, New York Representative Alexandria Ocasio-Cortez, and an impressive list of liberal and left-leaning VIPs back this idea.

There are different versions of the plan, but it boils down to this. The federal government must give everyone who wants to work a job that pays at least $15 an hour, offers benefits including health care and family leave, and would be "fitted" to the worker's skills and aptitudes. That is, the applicant would not have to demonstrate the skills required for a certain job. Instead, the person would be given a job that fits his or her skills and aptitude—guaranteed. As Professor Stephanie Kelton of Stony Brook University explained it:

---

[91] "The sheer size of our government workforce is an alarming problem." By Kristen Tate. *The Hill*, April 14, 2019. Viewed March 7, 2020. Accessible at https://thehill.com/opinion/finance/438242-the-federal-government-is-the-largest-employer-in-the-nation.

> *The aim "is not to change the worker in some fundamental way.... You take the worker the way they are and you fit the job to the worker.... You don't have to prove anything, you don't have to meet certain requirements. It's just an open-ended offer of employment for anyone seeking work...*[92]

A jobs guarantee is not a new idea. During the Great Depression, President Franklin Roosevelt pushed through legislation creating the Civilian Conservation Corps and other entities that put people to work. Once they were getting a paycheck, they had some hope. What the people did *not* get was a substantial, lasting improvement in the economy. The Great Depression didn't end until the U.S. entered World War II and the economy went into overdrive.

There are some obvious problems with this current job guarantee, including how to pay for it, how to find enough jobs that "fit" the workers, and how to inspire people to work diligently when their jobs are guaranteed. Proponents say the program might pay for itself by giving people more money to spend, thus reducing their reliance on welfare programs, and boosting the economy in general. But it's just as likely that this complex program might cost so much that the government ends up paying out a lot more than it saves.

How would a program like this pan out? There were just under 6 million unemployed people in January of 2020.[93]

---

[92] "What Is A Federal Jobs Guarantee?" By Laura Paddison. *HuffPost*, July 6, 2018. Viewed March 4, 2020. Accessible at https://www.huffpost.com/entry/federal-job-guarantee-explained_n_5b363f4ae4b007aa2f7f59fc.

[93] "The Unemployment Situation—January 2020." News Release from the Bureau of Labor Statistics, U.S. Department of Labor, February 7, 2020. Viewed March 4, 2020. Accessible at https://www.bls.gov/news.release/pdf/empsit.pdf.

Professor Kelton (quoted above), estimates there may be 16 to 17 million additional unemployed or underemployed people who would be interested in a guaranteed job.

For the sake of argument, let's say about 20 million apply. The federal government then has to come up with 20 million jobs that these folks are "fitted" to, no matter what their skills and aptitudes might be. So if 100,000 people "fitted" for work as clerical assistants apply in Houston, Texas, clerical assistant jobs must be found for them, whether or not the federal government actually needs 100,000 new clerical assistants in Houston. Because the jobs are guaranteed, these new employees can't be fired for doing a poor job, having a bad attitude, or not showing up. Or if they are fired, since work is guaranteed, they will have to be given another job.

Meanwhile, what happens to low-wage private businesses like fast-food places, amusement parks, movie theaters, and farms? It doesn't take a crystal ball to see that a lot of people will suddenly realize they're best "fitted" for some nice office job, not flipping burgers or strapping people into their seats on a roller coaster. I'm not knocking these folks, who would be following their interests. But a guaranteed jobs program would warp the labor market, forcing smaller enterprises to complete with the feds—which they won't be able to do. So what happens to business owners if they can no longer afford to hire employees and have to close up shop? Well, I guess they can always get a guaranteed government job. Of course, a whole lot of them are best "fitted" for opening and running small enterprises. Does this mean the federal government will have to go into the business of opening and running Burger Kings and nail salons?

A guaranteed jobs program is a bad idea for the workers and the country. Many of the workers will become weaker because they know their checks will arrive and benefits will flow, no matter how poor their performance.

In communist Czechoslovakia, everyone was guaranteed a job—so long as they did not anger the government—and most workers had little incentive to excel. Many became experts at sliding by. Eventually, Czechoslovakia had a hard time producing sufficient amounts of just about anything, even simple items like toilet paper.

Give Me the Bucks!

Some people believe that offering a "well-fitted" job to all who want one is not enough. They say that the federal government should just give money to everyone, via a Universal Basic Income. This is an old idea, currently supported by notables such as Bill Gates, Mark Zuckerberg, and many politicians. The idea is that everyone is given a fixed sum of money. The sum most often mentioned is $1,000 per month, and everyone receives it—rich, poor, homeless, executives, students, workers, CEOs, retired people, and people who are just lazing around.

Proponents of the plan believe it would help lift people out of generations of poverty, allow workers to quit their jobs and look for better ones, and make it easier for those who want to go back to school to do so. This extra cash cushion could also give people enough leisure time to create great art, enough extra cash to open new businesses, or enough freedom to hang out and just be themselves. It could help families by allowing someone to stay home and look after the kids. And it could improve the economy by putting more cash into circulation.

Opponents of the Universal Basic Income point out that it would be incredibly expensive: we're talking trillions-of-dollars expensive. In addition, dumping all of this cash into the economy would create serious inflation, driving up the prices of many items and seriously diminishing the buying power of that monthly $1,000. Worst of all, it would destroy incentive. While some might use the extra money to improve their skill sets, set aside money for retirement, or otherwise improve their lives, many people would spend more time *not* working, *not* improving their skill sets, *not* creating great art, and *not* opening new businesses.

Handing out "free money" has been tested in small ways in different countries, with mixed results. Sometimes it has positive effects, sometimes it does not. But all of the studies were small and short term, which limits their viability. The experts continue to debate the pros and cons of a Universal Basic Income, but I can tell you firsthand what it's like to live in a system that included such a plan (i.e., communism). As long as we didn't challenge the government, we had jobs for life that paid us wages, whether we worked hard or not. We had to sit there all day, but that didn't make us good workers. It just infantilized us, making us even more dependent on government hand-outs.

A guaranteed basic income would cause similar problems in this country. It would weaken the incentive of many to excel, or even try, at work.

It would make us less likely to contribute to our community and to those who are struggling. We would think: Why should we help out? Let them use their guaranteed money to take care of themselves.

We would become more disengaged from our nation, our heritage, our future. Why get involved in society and politics, or care about anything other than keeping the cash coming? For many, politics would amount to nothing more than pushing for "raises" and voting for the politicians who were offering us more.

It would give the government more and more power over our lives because whatever the government gives, it has the power to take away. And that gives it tremendous leverage over us.

I also believe it would most likely increase illegal immigration. You can be sure that as soon as the Universal Basic Income went into effect, some people would demand that it be extended to everyone present in the U.S., legally or otherwise. And once people in other parts of the world realized that all they had to do to get the monthly handout was cross our border, they'd spend all of their resources trying to get in.

Here are some better ideas: Instead of giving everyone $12,000 a year, how about making it easier for employers to hire people by taking the huge expense of employee health care off the backs of businesses? How about lowering the cost of employing people by reducing the employer's share of social security and other taxes? Or slashing burdensome regulations that make it so much easier and cheaper to use machines instead of people. How about streamlining the permit process, so more businesses can open? It makes much more sense to make it easier for people to earn a living than it does to make it easier for them to not work.

The "Give Me" Society

Give me a job! Give me a free place to live, free college, free health care, free money for life! Ask not about my purpose in life, or what I'm willing to work for—just gimme! And pass a law about those horrible "pink and blue" aisles in department stores! I just can't handle going into a store and seeing them!

One of the biggest problems with a "Give Me" society and getting things for free is it robs us of a sense of dignity and accomplishment. Work gives us purpose—and we need *more* purpose, not less. Another big problem is it's not "free"—someone, somewhere, has to pay for it and, undoubtedly, that's you and me, the taxpayers. And yet, so many of us are on board with this idea. Whatever we can grab, we do. If there are consequences, we'll think about them later.

This attitude is not only unfortunate, it's dangerous. President Kennedy once noted that, "Every time we try to lift a problem from our own shoulders, and shift that problem to the hands of the government... we are sacrificing the liberties of our people."[94] Yet in modern times, plenty of our problems have been shifted to the hands of the government. Today, we have housing subsidies and vouchers, low-income home energy assistance, welfare, supplemental security income, federal student grants and loans, earned income tax credits, school lunch programs, and unemployment insurance. There are programs such as Medicaid, Head Start, TANF (Temporary Assistance for Needy Families), SNAP (Supplemental Nutrition Assistance Program), and CHIP (Children's Health Insurance Program), to name just a few. On the federal, state, and local levels, we're spending billions and billions of dollars every year on assistance of all kinds.

And yet, if you listen to the people constantly clamoring for more, you can only conclude that this assistance has gone for naught. The truth is it will never be enough because when people rely on the government to support and guide them through life, they become weaker, lazier, less willing and able to take care of themselves, and more eager to put their fate into the hands of the government. And that requires the surrendering of their liberty and of their future.

[94] "Remarks of Representative John F. Kennedy at the Italian-American Charitable Society Dinner, Copley Plaza Hotel, Boston, MA, April 22, 1950." John F. Kennedy Presidential Library and Museum, undated. Viewed March 6, 2020. Accessible at https://www.jfklibrary.org/archives/other-resources/john-f-kennedy-speeches/boston-ma-italian-american-charitable-society-19500422.

Chapter Twelve

What the Government Gives, It Can Take

When I was living in communist Czechoslovakia, the government gave us a lot, including education, health care, and housing. But here's a hard truth that I learned: Once you take something from the government, it makes the rules.

Back then, if you did something the government didn't like, it could—and would—take away your job, your home, and your freedom to travel anywhere farther than a ten-mile radius from wherever you ended up living. Earlier, I told the story of my ex-husband David, whose parents tried, unsuccessfully, to defect from communist Czechoslovakia. First, the government threatened to send David to an orphanage, forcing his parents to come back home. Then, for several years, it stripped them of their apartment, their jobs, and their freedom to leave the area. There are other extreme examples of governmental giving and taking, such as communist China's punishment of those who don't follow certain societal rules, taking away "social points" that can lead to their being banned from using the bullet train or buying theater tickets.

In communism, a lack of concern with laws, morality, or historical norms makes it possible for takebacks to happen all the time. But the United States government also has the power to take back what it gives by withholding money, restricting rights, and welshing on promises of protection and security, just to name a few.

Why might our government take back what it gives to you? Some of the most common reasons are:

- it has made poor financial decisions;
- it wants to "save" the environment;
- it feels threatened;
- it wants to protect you from yourself;
- it wants to gain political advantage;

…and more. Let's take a closer look at some of the reasons why the government often takes back as readily as it gives.

The Government Takes When it Makes Poor Financial Decisions

First off, a confession: I'm not a big fan of the social security system. I believe it's wrong for the federal government to forcibly take money from our paychecks, promising that we'll be given money years later in the form of social security checks. I think most people are smart enough to save for their futures—and the primary reason we don't save nearly enough is that we've been fooled by governmental assurances that we'll be taken care of in our old age, through social security and other programs.

Still, I do believe that once the government has made a promise, it should stick to it. It should never go back on a commitment, even partially, because people are counting on it. Yet our government has already welshed on social security promises to some degree, and is poised to do so again in the near future.

Social security is based on the idea that today's workers (the "working generation") pay for today's retirees (the "retired generation"). This means that the money taken out of your paycheck is *not* set aside, put into an investment fund, and returned to you decades later. Instead, it's handed over to those who are retired to be spent now. Your own payout, theoretically, will come from those who are working once you have retired.

This approach worked well back in the 1930s, when social security began, because the working generation was much larger than the retired generation. But by the 1980s, the working generation had become a lot smaller relative to the retired generation, and the system was no longer sustainable. To counteract the government's poor financial decision, Congress decided to raise the standard retirement age from 65 to as high as 67, depending on the retiree's birth date. It was either that or drain the social security coffers dry.

This is a classic example of the government taking back what was given: in this case, a promise of payments to begin at a certain age. For decades, tens of millions of people had been counting on the government to honor that promise. Then, the promise was changed. And the promise is likely to change again because of the government's bad decisions when designing our social security system.

Eventually, the system is bound to collapse, mostly because of continuing demographic changes. As economics professor Walter E. Williams of George Mason University—whom I recently interviewed on the "RadioVice Online" podcast I cohost with Jim Vicevich—noted in 2011, "In 1940, there were 160 workers paying into Social Security per retiree; today, there are only 2.9 and falling."[95] Since Professor Williams wrote this, the ratio has dropped to 2.4 workers per retiree, and, apparently,

---

[95] "Social Security Disaster." By Walter E. Williams. WalterWilliams.com, October 5, 2011. Viewed February 3, 2020. Accessible at http://walterewilliams.com/social-security-disaster/.

the government has already spent the money that is supposed to be in a reserve fund. According to Professor Williams, the "Security trust fund consists of government IOUs that have no real value at all and probably are not even worth the paper upon which they are printed."[96]

At some point in the near future, the entire social security system will collapse. And that's when the government will completely take back its promise of helping Americans through their golden years. (And by the way, Medicare is facing the same financial cliff, which means the government will likely have to break another set of promises.[97])

Of course, the feds aren't the only culprits. The states are also forced to take back because of their own poor decisions. For example, states collect taxes and fees for the building and repair of roads and bridges. Many people don't mind paying these taxes and fees because they see the direct link between what they pay and what they get.

But some states take the money raised for highways and use it elsewhere because they've gotten into financial trouble. And rather than go to the people and explain what must be cut from the budget, or how much taxes will increase, the state government shifts money from the highway account to other accounts. Like magic, the problem is "fixed," although it usually comes back to bite them in the rear, as seen in this article about the situation in Pennsylvania:

---

[96] "Social Security Disaster." By Walter E. Williams. WalterWilliams.com, October 5, 2011. Viewed February 3, 2020. Accessible at http://walterewilliams.com/social-security-disaster/.

[97] "Medicare Financial Outlook Worsens." By Phil Galewitz. *Kaiser Health News*, June 5, 2018. Viewed January 29, 2020. Accessible at https://khn.org/news/medicare-financial-outlook-worsens/.

Pennsylvania Auditor General Eugene DePasquale announced the findings of an audit of the Department of Transportation (PennDOT). He says more than $4 billion dollars from the Motor License Fund that were meant for PennDOT projects has instead gone to the state police....[98]

My own state of Connecticut has been taxing gasoline sales for years to pay for transportation improvements, putting this money into a special transportation fund. Unfortunately, the fund is expected to go into the red within two or three years. To keep the transportation money flowing, our governor, Ned Lamont, came up with a plan to put toll booths at more than a dozen bridges in the state. The tolls could range as high as $7, depending on the size of the vehicle and whether or not it is registered in Connecticut. The tolls are expected to raise $21 billion over 10 years.

But the state is already undermining this fund. The governor has proposed a special income tax break for people in the $35,000 to $145,500 income range to compensate for what they would spend on tolls. That's very nice, but this tax break is taking money out of state coffers. That money will have to be replaced, and where do you think the state will look first? Don't be surprised if they decide to take money from the "toll fund" and move it to the general fund to compensate for the tax break—and then they'll act totally surprised when there isn't enough toll money to fix the roads.

---

[98] "PennDOT Audit Reveals Billions Diverted from Gas Tax Fund." By WNEP web staff. *WNEP News*, updated April 25, 2019. Viewed January 29, 2020. Accessible at https://wnep.com/2019/04/25/penndot-audit-reveals-billions-diverted-from-gas-tax-fund/.

This financial chicanery happens all the time, at all levels of government, when poor financial decisions are made. When the government can't pay the piper, the money, promises, or whatever else we were counting on disappears—replaced by new promises, of course.

It's hard to believe that this will ever change, that the government will suddenly begin to budget wisely, spend our money exactly as promised, and never welsh on its promises.

The Government Takes When It Wants to "Save" the Environment

I live with my fiancé on a small plot of land in beautiful Glastonbury, Connecticut, an idyllic New England town with houses dating back to the 1600s, a town green and beautiful trees everywhere. The Connecticut River flows nearby, and hundreds of little lakes and ponds dot the area.

We have a beautiful little pond in our backyard that is surrounded by overgrown and dead trees. I'd like to remove the ugly, potentially dangerous branches and trees, but I can't. That's because the State of Connecticut has taken back my rights as a property owner in the name of preserving the environment. Even if I'm willing to pay a lot of money to hire the most environmentally-conscious tree trimmer in all of New England, I must first get a permit from the state. But there's no guarantee I'll ever be granted that permit, for if some bureaucrat I never get to meet decides otherwise, I'm out of luck. And if it turns out there's one little snail or anything else on an endangered species list living in my trees, I'm out of luck.

Connecticut has very strict rules about ponds and other bodies of water. In some cases, not only are you not allowed to touch "their" water, you can't even build a pond of your own without a permit. That's right; you can't take *your* shovel, dig a hole on *your* property, and fill it with *your* water without government permission.

I agree that a certain amount of environmental protection makes sense. The Earth is our home; we don't want to destroy it. But how much? Which regulations make sense, and which are excessive, or so costly that they're not worth the price? How much freedom should the government be allowed to take from us in forcing us to comply with these regulations? And which regulations help you, but hurt your neighbor? For example, cities and states have been banning plastic straws to protect the environment. That's well and good, but it's been reported that people with certain disabilities need flexible plastic straws to drink out of cups. The straw ban has made life harder for them.[99]

Federal and state environmental regulations have been piling on top of each other for years. In 2016, the House Committee on Energy and Commerce reported that over the past thirty years, the federal Environmental Protection Agency "has been publishing several hundred new rules each year," including rules "that are not expressly authorized" by the relevant law. In other words, the bureaucrats have become a law unto their own. Since 2009, the committee noted, the "EPA has published approximately 3,900 final rules in the Federal Register... adding to thousands of existing rules and restrictions already issued by the agency."[100]

---

[99] "Why People With Disabilities Want Bans On Plastic Straws To Be More Flexible." By Tove Danovich and Maria Godoy. *NPR*, July 11, 2018. Viewed January 30, 2020. Accessible at https://www.npr.org/sections/thesalt/2018/07/11/627773979/why-people-with-disabilities-want-bans-on-plastic-straws-to-be-more-flexible.

[100] Majority Memorandum for July 6, 2016, Subcommittee on Energy and Power Hearing. Report regarding the hearing entitled "A Review of EPA's Regulatory Activity During the Obama Administration: Energy and Industrial Sectors." U. S. House of Representatives Committee on Energy and Commerce, June 30,

Many environmental and other regulations are helpful. But when no one really understands what is going on, bureaucrats are free to write rules that cost us money and can affect our lives in negative ways.

Unfortunately, the government has no incentive to clear up the confusion. Chaos is good for the government, for confusion prevents people from saying, "Wait a minute, these rules don't make sense" or "These rules take away my choices." Confusion is often the government's best friend, and our government is taking full advantage of its bosom buddie.

And remember: Each environmental regulation takes away a bit of our freedom. As the rules and regulations pile up, our freedom becomes harder and harder to find under those piles of papers.

The Government Takes When It Feels Threatened

Our government faces plenty of challenges from several sources, internal and external. Invariably, it tries to protect itself using the tools at hand. If it controls the flow of money, it will use dollars as weapons. If it can change laws in its favor, new laws will be pushed through the legislature. If it has influence over housing and jobs, your home and your job might be at risk. Be assured that the government will always look for ways to protect itself, even if it means taking back from people.

We've seen plenty of examples of this in the United States. The Sedition Act of 1798 was an early example of our government giving a promise, then taking it back when it felt threatened. In this case, it took back the guarantee of free speech, enshrined in the First Amendment to the Constitution.

2016. Viewed January 30, 2020. Accessible at https://docs.house.gov/meetings/IF/IF03/20160706/105153/HHRG-114-IF03-20160706-SD002.pdf.

At the time, there were two competing political parties, the Federalists and the Democratic-Republicans. President John Adams, a Federalist, was viciously attacked in the press by the Democratic-Republicans, led by Thomas Jefferson. To protect themselves, the Federalists pushed the Sedition Act through Congress, giving the federal government the power to prosecute, fine, and imprison anyone who printed "any false, scandalous and malicious writing against Congress or the president."[101] In other words, criticizing the Federalists was now akin to treason. Over a dozen journalists were put on trial under the Sedition Act, and many were tossed in jail. Fortunately, the Sedition Act expired in 1801, and the new president, Thomas Jefferson, pardoned those who had been imprisoned under the Act.

The Federalists and Democratic-Republicans no longer exist. But we still have fierce battles between political parties, with Democrats and Republicans fighting for control of the federal and state governments, as well as the Supreme Court and lower courts. Both parties feel they are involved in a life-and-death struggle for the future of this country and are willing to take bold steps to "save" the nation—and themselves, of course. But this is nothing new.

In the early 1960s, during the Kennedy administration, civil rights were a huge and contentious issue. As President Kennedy saw it, civil rights were a threat to his administration and the Democratic Party. After all, it was Democrats who controlled politics in the southern states, the area where the infamous "Jim Crow" restrictions on blacks were at their worst. Kennedy believed that backing civil rights might cause a rift in the Democratic Party and weaken his chances of reelection

---

[101] "The Founding Fathers of our limited government: Thomas Jefferson and the freedom of speech." By Timothy Snowball. Pacific Legal Foundation, July 24, 2019. Viewed February 1, 2020. Accessible at https://pacificlegal.org/the-founding-fathers-of-our-limited-government-thomas-jefferson-and-the-freedom-of-speech/.

in 1964. So he allowed the FBI to investigate and attempt to undermine the Reverend Martin Luther King, a classic example of taking back the rights of privacy granted to all American citizens.

In more recent years, the government has exercised its power to take against religious groups holding beliefs it finds offensive—that is, offensive to the people who vote for the party in power. For example, during the Obama administration, the IRS went after certain religious groups, threatening to revoke their tax-exempt status. (The Obama administration was Democratic, and the religious groups being threatened tended to support Republican ideals.) I'm not in favor of tax-exemptions, but this is a clear case of the government using its power to take against those who it feels are threatening.

The federal government uses money as leverage against states and cities that dare to challenge it over laws. In 1984, the federal government got into a quarrel with South Dakota over the state's drinking age: should it be twenty-one or nineteen? The federal government decided to withhold part of the state's allotment of federal highway funds to pressure South Dakota into complying.[102] In 2018, President Trump threatened to withhold federal funds from California, which was forcing certain health insurance programs to offer abortion coverage.

Hey, That's *Our* Money!

It's important to remember that the money the government threatens to withhold is *our* money, taken from us in the form of taxes. And that money was intended to benefit the people living in those states and cities to whom it was allotted. So we're not

[102] The issue was resolved by the U.S. Supreme Court in South Dakota v. Dole.

just fans in the stands cheering for our favorites as this political battle unfolds. Our money becomes the government's weapon, and we are the losers, no matter how it plays out.

The more power the government has, the greater its temptation to take back rights, promises, or other "gifts" it has granted, when it feels threatened. And this means you are more likely to become a target of this abuse because when the government is running scared, it won't be thinking about what's best for you.

My own story of a government take back continues. In our neighborhood, each house has a water well. Unfortunately, we recently learned that the underground water in our area is contaminated with uranium, pesticides, and radon. Evidently, there is so much uranium that I could probably make money bottling and selling it—although I'm sure I would need a government permit to sell my own water.

The city wanted to hook up our houses to the city water supply, which would involve digging up the street and laying big pipes underground, with smaller pipes branching off to each house. And that came with a big price tag: about $20,000 per house for the big pipes, plus extra for the little pipes running to the individual houses. In addition, we'd be tied to the municipal water supply, which would mean having to pay monthly fees and taxes forever, plus drinking the chlorine the government puts in the water.

I was in favor of everyone installing their own water filtration systems. Each family could decide which system and filters to use and how much they wanted to pay, without opening yet another door to government interference. But if the other people in the neighborhood wanted to pay for the installation of water pipes, we could all vote on it—an example of local democracy in action. I would be happy with either outcome.

Then the city council invited everyone in the neighborhood to come and offer opinions as to what we should do. Several people got up and spoke. And then, unbelievably, we were told that it didn't matter what we thought, the city council was going to make the decision, and it was in favor of the water pipes.

So we *will* be assessed $20,000 apiece for the big pipe, no matter what we think, no matter if we install our own filtering systems. Whatever happened to individual rights?

Governmental Giving *Always* Leads to Governmental Taking

We've been encouraged to think of our government as the source (or possible source) of lots of wonderful things—tax breaks, welfare, free healthcare, free college education, free fill-in-the-blank-with-all-your-favorite-things.

Some may even believe the government is sort of a perpetual Santa Claus. But just as Santa puts coal in your stocking if you haven't been good, the government can take back its goodies and its promises when it has made poor financial decisions, wants to "save" the environment, feels threatened, wants to exert its power, or for any number of other reasons.

The government has long taken away from us by gerrymandering voting districts, thus stealing away our right to select the representatives of our choosing.

It "takes back" the ability of some people to get into college or get government contracts, via affirmative action and minority set-asides.

It takes away our freedom of choice as a parent, forcing us to educate our children according to the approved curriculum, even if we home school our kids. It hampers our right to practice certain trades, via licensing requirements that often make absolutely no sense at all. (See chapter 14 for more on this.) It takes or is trying to take our freedom to own and use guns, to purchase a stripped-down and inexpensive health insurance policy, and so much more.

The simple truth is that we cannot merrily rely on the government to give us things. All we can be sure of is whatever the government gives, it can take. And it will take, without any concern for us.

We must stop relying on the government as a perpetual Santa Claus. Instead, we should rely on ourselves as much as possible, taking responsibility for our lives. We should trim the size of government, reduce bureaucracy, and cut back on what the government does. The smaller the government becomes, the "larger" each and every one of us will be.

Chapter Thirteen

The Covid Horse

An ancient Greek legend tells of the bloody siege of Troy, a city located in what is now western Turkey. When the Trojan prince, Paris, ran off with the beautiful Helen, wife of Menelaus, king of the Greek city of Sparta, the Greek cities marshaled their forces and went after Troy with a vengeance. For the next ten years, they tried their best to destroy the mighty citadel of Troy, only to be repulsed again and again. Finally, the Greeks decided upon a new strategy. So they built a gigantic horse out of wood, later known as the Trojan Horse. They dragged the horse to the gates of Troy early one morning and left it there as an offering to the goddess Athena. They then quickly boarded their ships and sailed away. But they didn't go far, for they intended to return that very night.

When the Trojans saw that the Greeks were gone and had left behind a fantastic offering, they were overjoyed. They opened the mighty gates to their city, dragged the horse in, and celebrated all day and into the wee hours of the night. When they finally fell into their beds, many of them quite drunk, the wily Greeks sprung their trap. You see, the horse was not an offering, but a hiding place for a small group of Greek warriors. And as soon as the Trojans fell asleep, the Greeks crept out of the horse and threw open the city gates. The rest of the Greek soldiers, having stealthily sailed back, were waiting just outside. They flooded into the city and attacked. By the next morning, Troy was totally destroyed. This legend is the source of the old adage "*Beware of Greeks bearing gifts,*" a warning that you should be wary about ulterior motives if someone suddenly treats you kindly.

I thought about the Trojan Horse as I sat down to write this chapter on March 25, 2020. Like many others, I am spending almost all of my time indoors because the Covid-19 coronavirus is spreading around the world like wildfire. As of today, the virus has infected a confirmed 438,000 people, including Britain's Prince Charles, and has killed 19,674 people.[103] About a quarter of the world's population is currently under lockdown or has been ordered to shelter in place.

In the United States, where testing has been slow to begin and is not nearly as comprehensive as health experts wish, there are currently 53,934 confirmed cases and 728 deaths.[104] Early this morning, after much wrangling, the White House and Senate agreed on a $2 trillion stimulus program[105] to keep the economy from crashing and help ensure that people have enough money to pay rent and buy food. The details of this program have not yet been released, and it must still be passed by the House of Representatives to become official.

I'll come back to this bill and the Trojan Horse soon. But meanwhile, I'd like to consider this question: Have we been

---

[103] "Coronavirus map: how Covid-19 cases are spreading across the world." By Pablo Gutierrez. *The Guardian*, March 25, 2020. Viewed March 25, 2020. Accessible at https://www.theguardian.com/world/ng-interactive/2020/mar/25/coronavirus-map-how-covid-19-cases-are-spreading-across-the-world.

[104] "Coronavirus in the U.S.: Latest Map and Case Count." By Mitch Smith, Karen Yourish, Sarah Almukhtar, Keith Collins, Danielle Ivory, Allison McCann, Jin Wu and Amy Harmon. *New York Times*, updated March 25, 2020. Viewed March https://www.nytimes.com/interactive/2020/us/coronavirus-us-cases.html. Accessible at https://www.nytimes.com/interactive/2020/us/coronavirus-us-cases.html.

[105] "White House, Senate reach historic $2 trillion stimulus deal amid growing coronavirus fears." By Manu Raju, Ted Barrett, Clare Foran and Kristin Wilson. *CNN*, March 25, 2020. Viewed March 25, 2020. Accessible at https://www.cnn.com/2020/03/25/politics/stimulus-senate-action-coronavirus/index.html.

wise in allowing the government to have seized so much control over our nation's health system over the past many decades?

How Has It Come to This?

Americans are scared, and it's no wonder. They've been hearing for weeks about the lack of Covid virus testing kits, the paucity of hospital beds and ventilators, and the terrible strain our medical system will undergo when sick people start flooding the hospitals. They wonder if they'll wind up lying ignored in a hospital hallway without enough medicine or ventilators to treat them. Will the disease curve have flattened enough when their turn comes around? Will there be enough healthy doctors and nurses left to treat everyone?

How did we get to this point? The Covid-19 pandemic isn't a bolt out of the blue. We've long been aware of the danger of pandemics. We know exactly what happened with the H1N1 "swine flu" in 2009, SARS in 2003, and other diseases that have swept over national borders. We've known about the Covid virus since it began killing people in China in January 2020, so we've had time to get preparations under way. Yet the entire country is currently in a panic, buying toilet paper, sanitary wipes, and bottled water as if we'll never get another chance, while simultaneously hoping there will be a ventilator available if we should need it.

Many people are clamoring for federal government action. This is no surprise, for we've been conditioned to turn to Uncle Sam at the slightest sign of danger. And yet, long-standing government policies restricted the ability of our health-care system to respond to crises long before Covid-19 appeared.

Take, for example, the lack of hospital beds. You might think that the hospitals decide how many beds and other things they will need, based on community needs. Yet in New York, Florida, Georgia, Illinois, Kentucky, and many other states, they can't make that decision. That's because "certificate of need" (CON) laws, or variations on them, affect hospitals in about 35 of our 50 states. The CON laws, which date back to the 1960s, prohibit existing hospitals from adding beds or offering new health-care services as they think necessary. Neither can a new hospital simply open its doors. Instead, existing and new hospitals are required to demonstrate to the state government a "need" for additional beds and services. As a 2019 article in *Managed Healthcare Executive* pointed out. "The CON process can be required for both small and large investments: from hospital beds and gamma knives to new hospitals and neonatal intensive care units."[106]

In Hawaii, for example, CON approval is needed before you can offer or expand nearly 30 different health-care services, "including ultrasounds, MRIs, open-heart surgery, hospice, dialysis, neonatal intensive care, organ transplants, and obstetrics services."[107] The federal government worked hard to extend the CON laws, at one point requiring states to adopt them if they received certain federal funds.

Proponents of CON insist they improve the quality of health care. Restricting the number of hospitals, hospital beds, and other services, they say, means the existing hospitals in any given area will operate at full capacity. With plenty of patients to treat, hospital staff will gain experience, and the overall

---

[106] "Do Certificate-of-Need Laws Still Make Sense in 2019?" By Matthew Mitchell. *Managed Healthcare Executive*, September 23, 2019. Viewed March 27, 2020. Accessible at https://www.managedhealthcareexecutive.com/article/do-certificate-need-laws-still-make-sense-2019.

[107] "'Certificate of need' laws are certifiably unnecessary." By Malia Blom. *The Hill*, November 27, 2017. Viewed March 27, 2020. Accessible at https://thehill.com/opinion/healthcare/361971-certificate-of-need-laws-are-certifiably-unnecessary.

quality of healthcare will improve. This sounds reasonable: lots of patients means lots of practice for the doctors, nurses, and technicians, which leads to better skills. But has that really happened?

The answer is no, according to a 2016 study conducted by George Mason University's Mercatus Center. Instead, CON laws actually *lowered* the quality of care for many people:

> *The average 30-day mortality rate for patients with pneumonia, heart failure, and heart attack who were discharged from hospitals in CON states was 2.5–5 percent higher than that of their non-CON-state counterparts. The largest difference is in deaths following a serious postsurgery complication, with an average of six more deaths per 1,000 patient discharges...*[108]

Why would CON lower the quality of care? Because it reduces competition. The existing hospitals have less competition, which means they have less pressure to sharpen skills. They also have less need to please patients, or the insurance companies and government programs that pay the lion's share of the bills. Thus, the hospitals can get a bit sloppy, yet still have plenty of patients and still bring in plenty of money.

Proponents of CON also claim that restricting the number of hospital beds in any one area helps keep health spending down. But this flies in the face of economic reality: having

---

[108] "Certificate-of-Need Laws and Hospital Quality." By Thomas Stratmann. Mercatus Center, George Mason University, September 27, 2017. Viewed March 16, 2020. Accessible at https://www.mercatus.org/publications/corporate-welfare/certificate-need-laws-and-hospital-quality.

more of something and *increased* competition reduces costs. If CON reduces costs, then why do our health bills keep going up?

The truth is that CON is all about controlling competition and keeping the cash flowing in. The fewer the hospital beds, the more a hospital can charge for each one. This is the reason that one hospital may file an objection if a neighboring hospital submits a CON request to add more beds, or open a new wing offering, say, neonatal or cancer care. The first hospital doesn't want the additional competition because it will hurt their bottom line. Meanwhile, state governments love CON because it allows them to expand, write more regulations, and exert more control over our lives.

All of this might be tolerable if the bureaucrats got it right. That is, if they accurately calculated the number of hospitals and hospital beds needed in every area, plus a generous reserve for emergencies such as the current Covid-19 crisis. But that's not the case. Because of CON and other government regulations, the United States has only 2.8 hospital beds per 1,000 people. By comparison, South Korea has 12.3 hospital beds per 1,000 persons.[109] Italy has 3.2 beds per 1,000 people—which turned out to be a woefully inadequate number for servicing the tidal wave of people suffering from Covid virus in their country. At the moment, some Italian hospitals have absolutely no room for new patients,[110] while the people continue to get sicker and sicker.

---

[109] Data on hospital beds in this paragraph taken from "This is the coronavirus math that has experts so worried: Running out of ventilators, hospital beds." By William Wan, Ariana Eunjung Cha and Lena H. Sun. *Washington Post*, March 13, 2020. Viewed March 16, 2020. Accessible at https://www.washingtonpost.com/health/2020/03/13/coronavirus-numbers-we-really-should-be-worried-about/.

[110] "'Not a wave, a tsunami.' Italy hospitals at virus limit." By Nicole Winfield. *PBS*, March 13, 2020. Viewed March 16, 2020. Accessible at https://www.pbs.org/newshour/health/not-a-wave-a-tsunami-italy-hospitals-at-virus-limit.

Other Ways Government Has Hampered Health Care

Health care practitioners are licensed by the states: doctors in California are licensed to practice by California, doctors in Oklahoma are licensed by Oklahoma, and so on. A doctor is only allowed to practice medicine in the state where she was licensed. She can't pick up, move to another state, and begin caring for patients unless she gets a new license, which takes time and effort. Is this really necessary? Do germs change when they cross state lines? Is there a Florida flu and a Pennsylvania flu? These state licensing laws are so restrictive that health care practitioners can't even give it away for free in other states. As a 2017 report by the CATO Institute pointed out:

> *Volunteer groups such as Remote Area Medical have had to turn away patients or cancel free clinics in California, Florida, and Georgia because those states' licensing laws did not allow clinicians licensed by other states to give away free care.*[111]

Most people have no idea how much the government has restricted our medical care through CON, occupational licensing for health care providers, and other means. And since our insurance policies generally restrict our ability to "doctor shop" or "hospital shop," we have no incentive to find out. Neither do we have the incentive to look into government regulations restricting the production and use of health supplies and equipment. For example, as Covid-19 began spreading around the world,

---

[111] CATO Handbook For Policymakers. 35. Health Care Regulation. Viewed March 18, 2020. Accessible at https://www.cato.org/cato-handbook-policymakers/cato-handbook-policy-makers-8th-edition-2017/health-care-regulation.

health experts realized we needed a quick and reliable test kit to determine who had the disease. So the Centers for Disease Control (CDC) developed and began sending out a test kit on February 5, about two weeks after the first confirmed case of Covid in the U.S. Unfortunately, there were problems with the kit. But due to regulations concerning who can produce and distribute these kits, the faulty government kit remained the only game in town. Some universities developed their own test kits, but they couldn't distribute them unless they first got an Emergency Use Authorization from the FDA. But getting the Emergency Use Authorization took a fair amount of time, even in the midst of this huge, worldwide emergency. Initially, laboratories were even required to mail in a physical copy of their Emergency Use Authorization request to the government. Email wasn't good enough for our bureaucrats, who insisted on snail-mail! As of early March, a month after the first U.S. Covid patient was identified, and about three months after the crisis reared its ugly head in China, only about 2,000 Americans had been tested.[112]

I'm not criticizing the CDC scientists whose early test did not work well, for it often takes numerous tries to get it right. The problem is the endless government regulation, which tied the hands of some very smart people who wanted to help with the kits, even as the numbers of infections and deaths rose.

A Covid Horse?

With the Covid virus wreaking havoc on the economy, people and businesses have been clamoring for the federal government

---

[112] "Exclusive: The Strongest Evidence Yet That America Is Botching Coronavirus Testing." By Robinson Meyer and Alexis C. Madrigal. *Atlantic*, March 6, 2020. Viewed March 25, 2020. Accessible at https://www.theatlantic.com/health/archive/2020/03/how-many-americans-have-been-tested-coronavirus/607597/.

to assist by extending unemployment benefits, reducing payroll taxes, increasing Medicare funding, halting evictions, and so on. This has led to the federal government taking various measures, including the highly-anticipated $2 trillion relief bill just passed by the Senate and on its way to the House of Representatives for approval.

Even though I'm opposed to government expansion, a temporary, laser-focused relief bill might be appropriate during this severe emergency. Unfortunately, it is highly doubtful that the government will 1) act with wisdom and restraint in selecting the key interventions, 2) expand for only as long as necessary to help us through the crisis, and 3) shrink down once the crisis has passed.

The handwriting is already on the wall. For example, the initial Covid virus appropriations bill announced by Speaker of the House Nancy Pelosi contained, among other things, $35 million to support the Kennedy Center for the Performing Arts in Washington, D.C.; language strengthening airplane emission requirements; and a requirement for diversity on corporate boards.[113] Her bill also forced all businesses to provide employees with seven days of paid sick leave—forever. And employees would not have to use sick days to get tested or treated for Covid virus. Instead, they could take the paid time off for other reasons, including, as the text clearly stated, to deal with stalking, sexual assault, and domestic violence, or to help a friend deal with these issues.[114]

---

[113] "Most Politicians Are Disingenuous Opportunists. The Coronavirus Outbreak Only Makes That More Obvious." By Eric Boehm. *Reason*, March 25, 2020. Viewed March 25, 2020. Accessible at https://reason.com/2020/03/25/most-politicians-are-disingenuous-opportunists-the-coronavirus-outbreak-only-makes-that-more-obvious/.

[114] "Dems Want to Combat Coronavirus By Mandating Paid Leave for Stalking Victims?" By Billy Binion. *Reason*, March 12, 2020. Viewed March 16, 2020.

While Nancy Pelosi tries to slip stalking, domestic violence, and sexual assault into a Covid virus appropriations bill, others are attempting to do similar things. Some have suggested that the relief bill should force businesses to pay a minimum wage of $15 an hour and offer paid vacations—forever—and more. So our politicians are working hard to turn a virus appropriations bill into a Covid Horse. The bill will look wonderful from the outside, with relief money for many, but it's likely to be full of nasty surprises that curtail our freedom—it's expected to be about 800 pages long, which means there's plenty of "hiding spaces" for politicians' pet projects. And I seriously doubt it will contain a sunset clause that erases all of the new laws, rules, regulations, and bailouts it's created, once the emergency has passed.

Time to Say Goodbye?

Many industries have been hard hit by the economic slowdown, including hospitality, tourism, and retail. They are asking the government for aid. Just one industry, airlines, has asked for $54 billion in federal grants, unsecured loans, and tax cuts.[115] But before we taxpayers hand over piles of dough to the airlines, let's not forget they are advised by top-notch accountants and have had plenty of opportunity to plan for future crises. Despite this, they have not been setting aside funds for emergencies. Instead, over the past several years, airlines have been "stockpiling

---

Accessible at https://reason.com/2020/03/12/dems-want-to-combat-coronavirus-by-mandating-paid-sick-leave-for-stalking-victims/.

[115] "Here's the exact $54 billion bailout plan that airlines are demanding of the US government as coronavirus wreaks havoc on the industry." By Graham Rapier. *Business Insider*, March 16, 2020. Viewed March 16, 2020. Accessible at https://www.businessinsider.com/coronavirus-airlines-bailout-proposal-congress-trump-white-house-2020-3.

debt and spending billions to drive up stock prices through buybacks. American Airlines has spent about $12.4 billion on stock repurchases since 2014. Southwest has spent $10.7 billion buying back stock."[116]

A stock buyback occurs when a company purchases shares of its own stock from investors. This is good for investors if the stock price is high because they can make a profit. It's also good for the companies because it consolidates their ownership and pumps up the price of their shares. Stock buybacks are standard and often a good idea. But notice that American and Southwest spent about $23 billion between them on stock buybacks in the past six years. Shouldn't they have squirreled at least some of that $23 billion away, as a reserve for future problems?

While American, Southwest, and other airlines were spending tens of billions of dollars on buybacks, they've also been piling on the debt. According to Barron's, Delta Air Lines is currently about $17 billion in debt, United Airlines Holdings $20.5 billion, and American Airlines Group $33.4 billion.[117] The very highly-paid financial wizards who advise these companies know that this kind of debt leaves very little room to maneuver in a time of crisis. Yet just three airlines—Delta, United, and American—have amassed about $70 billion in debt. If they had not racked up all that debt, they wouldn't need to ask the government for $54 billion.

---

[116] "American Airlines spent $12 billion on stock buybacks during flush times. Now it says it needs a bailout." By Kyle Arnold. *Dallas Morning News*, March 18, 2020. Viewed March 19, 2020. Accessible at https://www.dallasnews.com/business/airlines/2020/03/18/american-airlines-spent-12-billion-on-stock-buybacks-during-flush-times-now-it-says-it-needs-a-bailout/.

[117] "Airline Stocks Have Gotten Crushed by Coronavirus. They're Not All the Same." By Nicholas Jasinski and Al Root. *Barron's*, updated March 14, 2020. Viewed March 19, 2020. Accessible at https://www.barrons.com/articles/airline-stocks-arent-a-buy-yet-heres-watch-to-watch-for-51584145003.

When your business strategy is based on incurring huge debt while giving money back to your shareholders, and then running to the government crying for a handout when trouble strikes, something is wrong. And when something is this rotten, I say it's time to let it go. The big airlines will not change their ways, and we'll be asked to prop them up, over and over again, forever. I'll personally dig a grave for them, using a shovel made of their old iron-clad promises to behave themselves in exchange for previous bailouts—promises which turned out to be worthless. Meanwhile, even as we're bidding farewell to the failed airlines, the government should cut back on bureaucratic red tape, on overly burdensome rules and regulations, and make it easier for new airlines to spring up to replace the old, for existing smaller carriers to expand.

Of course, it's not just the airline industry that's piled on debt then run to the government for help. Many other industries have also behaved with reckless financial abandon in recent years, and now have very little in reserve to weather the crisis. According to Barron's:

> *Corporate debt as a percentage of gross domestic product is now at "the highest peak we've ever had," says Edward Altman, professor emeritus of finance at New York University Stern School of Business...*[118]

In November of 2019, before the onslaught of the Covid virus, the International Monetary Fund, the U.S. Federal Reserve, and others issued warnings about this level of debt:

---

[118] "The Coronavirus Crisis Could Wipe Out Entire Industries. These Are the Ones at Risk." By Avi Salzman. *Barron's*, March 20, 2020. Viewed March 25, 2020. Accessible at https://www.barrons.com/articles/these-debt-heavy-industries-stand-to-fare-worst-during-the-virus-crisis-51584742383.

> *"We are sitting on the top of an unexploded bomb, and we really don't know what will trigger the explosion," said Emre Tiftik, a debt specialist at the Institute of International Finance...*[119]

Well, it looks like the bomb has exploded, its fuse lit by the Covid virus. Yet it seems unlikely that the government will take strong measures during this time because people feel it's only natural for businesses and entire industries to turn to the government for help in times of crisis. Even though we've seen, too often, that this "help" is usually nothing more than an expensive, short-term fix, it will happen. And businesses will continue to beg for more, like addicts who can't face the world without a fix. The government is both their poison and the reason they will continue to behave irresponsibly.

Time to Restore Capitalism

While we're bidding *adieu* to irresponsible companies, let's ask ourselves if it's wise for the government to continue wielding such power over our health care system. The system was limping along before Covid appeared, burdened by reams of regulations, and when the Covid crisis hit, the systemic flaws most of us never thought about were instantly revealed. It's time to slash away the forest of laws and regulations and free the health system. Let's allow hospitals to build the beds they believe are necessary, and allow doctors and nurses

[119] "Corporate debt nears a record $10 trillion, and borrowing binges poses new risks." By David Lynch. *Washington Post*, November 29, 2019. Viewed March 26, 2020. Accessible at https://www.washingtonpost.com/business/economy/corporate-debt-nears-a-record-10-trillion-and-borrowing-binge-poses-new-risks/2019/11/29/1f86ba3e-114b-11ea-bf62-eadd5d11f559_story.html.

licensed in one state to practice in another. Let's cut through the restrictions that made it so difficult for doctors and nurses to use non-approved masks—masks which often turned out to be fine once the regulations were waived. Let's make it easier for universities and industry to create new tests, medicines, and other devices. And while we're at it, let's start leveling the mountains of regulations, taxes, and fees that make it so difficult for industry to survive in this country. As you recall, when the Covid crisis began, health experts pointed out that we're dependent on other countries for many of our medicines and much of our health-care equipment.

On March 25, this headline appeared on CNN: "The US is asking other countries for everything from hand sanitizer to ventilators to help fight the coronavirus."[120] The article notes that U.S. hospitals are requesting a variety of items, including "biohazard bags, N-95 masks, gloves, gowns, surgical caps, shoe covers, sharps containers, protective eyewear, hand sanitizer and Tyvek suits.... metered dose inhalers, ventilators, elastomeric respirators and powered air purifying respirators."

If we were to jettison many of the burdensome rules that have driven so much of our industry overseas, and cut back on unnecessary regulations, we would likely be producing plenty of pharmaceuticals, masks, and other necessary items right here.

There is no reason why this nation should have to go begging. But we do, because the current system has failed. It failed because we allowed ourselves to believe that bureaucrats could run our health care system for us. It's time for us to stop

---

[120] "The US is asking other countries for everything from hand sanitizer to ventilators to help fight the coronavirus." By Nicole Gaouette. *CNN*, March 25, 2020. Viewed March 26, 2020. Accessible at https://www.cnn.com/2020/03/25/politics/us-global-appeal-corona-supplies/index.html.

believing that someone else will make our problems magically vanish, and to take back control of our own health care system.

The government has been expanding its control over the health care system for decades, and telling us that this is for our own good. In a sense, they imply, it's their gift to us. Well, next time you read about bureaucrats wanting to take more control of the health system for the benefit of the people, remember what happened when the people of Troy were given their "gift."

Chapter Fourteen

The Freedom Spectrum: Trending Toward Red?

Socialism, like so many things, exists on a spectrum: the freedom spectrum. On one end of the spectrum is total freedom, and on the other end is complete socialism. On the freedom end, we have private firms that own their own assets; prices that are determined by supply and demand; limited taxes and limited government spending on public services; health care that's purchased on the free market; and personal income that's tied to market forces. On the socialism end, we have assets that are owned by the government or "the people"; prices that are controlled by the government; increased taxes and higher governmental spending on public services; government-provided health care; and personal income that's redistributed by the government to the people to make everyone "equal."

How can you determine where we currently land on the freedom-versus-socialism spectrum? Here's an easy, three-step way to gauge it: 1) The more money you're required to give to the government, 2) the more enforced contact you have with the government, and 3) the more your everyday behavior is dictated by the government, the higher the level of socialism in your society and the less freedom you have.

Increases in taxes, enforced contact with the government, and government-dictated behavior are the forerunners of socialism. And they are very much on the rise in the United States. Let's take a look at these three indicators, beginning with the money.

Freedom Eroded a Dollar at a Time

Every time you pay taxes to support a government program—above and beyond those needed to ensure our safety and security—you surrender a little bit of your personal liberty. That's because every dollar that leaves your pocket and lands in government hands erodes your freedom to decide how that money should be spent. Suddenly it's theirs, and they have all the power.

You might be okay with some of this. For example, you might enjoy the arts and wish that someone would support them. But every time you are *required* to give the government a dollar to fund the arts, you have a dollar less to support the art of your choice.

Similarly, you might feel bad for people in other countries who lack houses or go to bed hungry. But every time you are *required* to give the government a dollar for foreign aid, you have a dollar less to donate to the country of your choice, or to needy people in your own community. Or to invest for yourself to make sure you always have enough to eat and a place to live.

Even if you agree with the ways your money is being used, *the government* is spending your money, not you. The government decides which groups or individuals get the funds, and how they can use them. It determines who will be hired, how much they will be paid, whether or not to give hiring preference to members of "disadvantaged groups," and how carefully to monitor the work that's done. You, personally, have no power to make any of these choices. And if you refuse to give the government the cash it demands, you may lose your freedom completely.

How Many Dollars' Worth of Freedom Do We Surrender?

According to USAspending.gov, the federal government spent $4.45 trillion of our money in 2019.[121] This figure doesn't include all of the money spent by the states, counties/parishes, cities, and special entities like school and fire districts. This avalanche of money is *ours*, yours and mine, because the government can't earn a salary on its own. The only way it can fill its coffers is by taking money out of *our* pockets.

For example, in my state of Connecticut in 2019, we citizens were on the hook for almost $22 billion to fund the first year of our new two-year $43 billion dollar budget.[122] Add to this the approximately $165 million spent by my hometown of Glastonbury, plus what we fork over to the feds, and you can see we surrender a lot of freedom in the form of dollars to the government.

Now, Connecticut is a small state, and Glastonbury is a small town, home to fewer than 35,000 people. Just think of how much freedom the people in big states and huge cities like New York, Chicago, and Los Angeles are forced to surrender. To give you a rough idea, the latest budget for New York State is in the neighborhood of $175 billion, and for New York City, it's about $93 billion.[123] That means that people who live in New York City are forced to participate in the loss of $268 billion

---

[121] USAspending.gov. No author listed. Undated. Viewed January 16, 2020. Accessible at https://www.usaspending.gov/#/.

[122] "Senate approves two-year $43, billion state budget; Gov. Lamont expect to sign." by Christopher Keating. *Hartford Courant*, June 4, 2019. Viewed January 16, 2020. Accessible at https://www.courant.com/politics/hc-pol-senate-budget-vote-tuesday-20190604-rlazqvwporemnb7tavr4not7jm-story.html.

[123] "5 Takeaways From New York City's $93 Billion Budget Deal." By William Neuman. *New York Times*, June 15, 2019. Viewed January 16, 2020. Accessible at https://www.nytimes.com/2019/06/15/nyregion/nyc-budget-funding.html.

dollars' worth of freedom a year—and that's not counting what they have to give to the federal government, the county, and any special districts.

Some people might say that we volunteer to pay the taxes necessary to run the government because taxes are set by the politicians we elected and the bureaucrats who they, in turn, appoint. And while it's true that politicians do determine tax levels, most of them also carve out special tax breaks for the companies and industries that give them big donations. These are the same politicians who probably got elected by promising us they would not raise our taxes. They certainly didn't win their seats by hitting the campaign trail and announcing, "I'm going to *raise* the taxes of everyone in this state by $5,000 apiece!" even if they knew this would probably be the case.

Usually, they mislead us with false promises, like free health care or free college education for everyone. Naturally, if any of these things come to pass, they will be paid for with your hard-earned dollars, and cost you even more in the form of freedom lost.

Chained to Uncle Sam

The second indicator of the slide toward socialism is increasing, enforced contact with the government. We're all forced to deal with the government by paying taxes, doing jury duty, applying for passports and driver's licenses, and so on. This is a fact of life in a well-ordered society.

However, when enforced contact with the government becomes excessive or is required for ridiculous reasons, it's time to wonder if socialism is starting to become the norm. Let's look, for example, at state requirements that those who work in certain professions be licensed in order to work legally.

Many people would argue that some practitioners should be licensed. We would, for example, like to know that the doctor who is slicing us open on the operating table or prescribing powerful medicines has gone through a rigorous, well-defined training program, and can tell an aspirin from a statin. We might also like the idea that contractors and electricians be licensed, so our houses don't fall down or catch fire. Perhaps attorneys as well, for a crappy attorney can cost us a lot of money, or put up a weak fight when the government tries to throw us in jail.

But in some states, the list of professions that require licenses has ballooned to ridiculous size, and includes "locksmiths, ballroom dance instructors, hair braiders, manicurists, interior designers, and upholsterers."[124] The State of Massachusetts requires licenses for fortune-tellers,[125] and Louisiana has required florists to be licensed since 1950.[126]

Florists? What horrible danger do we face from unlicensed florists? While I might need a well-trained doctor to figure out the source of my chest pain, I can usually decide for myself whether I want roses or carnations. In Hartford, Connecticut, it's illegal for anyone to collect "rags, paper, glass, old metal, junk, cinders or other waste matter in the city" without a

---

[124] "Nearly 30 Percent of Workers in the U.S. Need a License to Perform Their Job: It Is Time to Examine Occupational Licensing Practices." By David Hershbein, David Boddy, and Melissa S. Kearney. Brookings, January 27, 2015. Viewed January 18, 2020. Accessible at https://www.brookings.edu/blog/up-front/2015/01/27/nearly-30-percent-of-workers-in-the-u-s-need-a-license-to-perform-their-job-it-is-time-to-examine-occupational-licensing-practices/.

[125] "How do you license a fortune teller?" By Paul Debole. *Commonwealth*, October 30, 2018. Viewed January 30, 2020. Accessible at https://commonwealthmagazine.org/opinion/how-do-you-license-a-fortune-teller/.

[126] "Do You Have a License for That Bouquet?" By Danny Heitman. *Wall Street Journal*, August 24, 2018. Viewed January 18, 2020. Accessible at https://www.wsj.com/articles/do-you-have-a-license-for-that-bouquet-1535147773.

license. So, if you're in the market to collect junk in Hartford, you'd better hightail it down to city hall first.[127]

These examples might sound like ridiculous bureaucracy that we can safely ignore. Unfortunately, people can get in serious trouble for scoffing at such laws or trying to get around them. In 2017, the State of Tennessee hauled a barber named Elias Zarate into court for practicing barbering without a license.[128] Zarate had learned to cut hair as a kid, in his uncle's barbershop. He knew how to do it well, he had experience, his clients were happy, but he couldn't get a barbering license in Tennessee because he didn't have the high school degree necessary for licensure. He ended up buying a fake license and got busted for barbering without a valid license. Zarate was fined $1,500 plus an additional $600 to cover court costs and other fees.

I certainly wouldn't advise anyone to break the law by barbering without a license. But I do wonder if you need to take high school courses in algebra, European history, chemistry, and the rest in order to give someone a decent haircut. I, for one, have never discussed the causes and consequences of the English Civil War with any of my hairdressers!

Here's another example of a silly license. Pardon me for picking on Tennessee again, but if you want to massage horses, that state requires you to be a veterinarian.[129] The state is quite strict about this and sent what amounted to "cease and desist"

---

[127] Hartford, Connecticut–Code of Ordinances/Chapter 19–JUNK COLLECTORS AND RAGPICKERS. Viewed January 23, 2020. Accessible at: https://library.municode.com/ct/hartford/codes/code_of_ordinances?nodeId=PTIIMUCO_CH19JUCORA.

[128] "Tennessee's Haircut Cops Bust Barbers Who Lack High School Diplomas." By Eric Boehm. *Reason*, January 19, 2018. Viewed January 23, 2020. Accessible at https://reason.com/2018/01/19/barber-cops-bust-high-school-dropouts/.

[129] "This Ridiculous Occupational Licensing Law is Hurting Local Entrepreneurs." By Brittany Hunter. Center for Individualism, April 12,

letters to two Tennessee women who had the nerve to massage a horse without a vet's degree.

One is Laurie Wheeler, who holds a certificate in equine myofascial release, a type of massage used for performance horses. She also holds a license in massage therapy for humans. You'd think that with these qualifications the state would let her help out some horses—especially since she was doing it for free. Nope. She received an official letter telling her she was breaking the law and could be fined and arrested.

According to the State of Tennessee, it would be very simple for Laurie Wheeler to get on the right side of the law so she could massage horses legally. Just spend four years in veterinarian school, while going into horrendous debt to cover the tuition. Or she could help horses in a different way, for the state actually allows you to castrate and/or artificially inseminate horses without a license. You know, it may just be me, but if offered a choice between unlicensed massage and unlicensed insemination, I'd go for the massage.

Does the Licensing Mania Really Protect Us?

The number of jobs requiring licenses has expanded tremendously in recent decades. Whereas about 5% of workers required an occupational license in 1960, today over 20% of workers must have one, or they are not allowed to work. In fact, some 1,100 different occupations require a license in one or more states.

Do we really need so many people to be licensed? Is there really a danger that workers in all 1,100 occupations might harm us if the state doesn't diligently license them? And just how diligent are they when setting the requirements for these licenses?

2018. Viewed January 23. Accessible at https://centerforindividualism.org/the-most-ridiculous-occupational-licensing-law-youve-ever-heard/.

According to an article published in the *Harvard Business Review*,[130] in 2012, the education/training required to be licensed as an optician was 1,128 days in Nevada, but zero days in neighboring California. And while opticians in Connecticut had to pass four examinations, those in Vermont only had to pass one. So which do we need, zero days or 1,128, one exam or four?

If excellence is really the goal when setting licensing standards, why is it that "Michigan requires 1,460 days of education and training to become an athletic trainer, but just 26 to be an emergency medical technician (EMT). In fact, across all states, interior designers, barbers, cosmetologists, and manicurists all face greater average licensing requirements than do EMTs."[131] Who do you want to be better trained, the person picking your living room couch or the one shocking your heart with electric paddles because you just had a massive heart attack? Given the crazily inconsistent requirements for licenses from state to state, we really can't be sure that everyone with a license is truly qualified.

Even when the idea behind licensing makes sense, even when the educational/training requirements are realistic, and even when the licensing fees are reasonable, licenses stifle competition. That's because the harder it is for new people to enter the field, the more business there is for those already in

---

[130] "More and More Jobs Today Require a License. That's Good for Some Workers, but Not Always for Consumers." By Edward Timmons. *Harvard Business Review*, April 26, 2018. Viewed January 18, 2020. Accessible at https://hbr.org/2018/04/more-and-more-jobs-today-require-a-license-thats-good-for-some-workers-but-not-always-for-consumers.

[131] "More and More Jobs Today Require a License. That's Good for Some Workers, but Not Always for Consumers." By Edward Timmons. *Harvard Business Review*, April 26, 2018. Viewed January 18, 2020. Accessible at https://hbr.org/2018/04/more-and-more-jobs-today-require-a-license-thats-good-for-some-workers-but-not-always-for-consumers.

the field. This explains why professional associations generally support more stringent licensing requirements—it keeps the pool of competitors smaller.

Certification is another story. While a license is legally mandatory, a certificate is generally voluntary, a "badge of excellence" that many workers want to earn. It sets them above non-certified workers and may allow them to charge higher fees. I don't think interior designers, for example, should be required to get a license. But if some put in the extra effort to obtain a certificate in interior design, then I have the choice of using them and paying extra because I think they will provide superior service.

In short, the government's involvement in the licensing of way too many occupations often doesn't make a difference to our safety. But it always works against competition, and competition is one of the driving forces behind capitalism. Lack of competition is a hallmark of socialism.

By the way, if you feel the need to license someone, how about all those talking heads on television who can mislead us, turn our children against their country, and influence elections? They can spew all the fake news and lies they want, can twist the facts, and mock people with impunity. They have a huge amount of power. If we're really worried about protecting this country, maybe we should demand that they get an occupational "license to persuade."

Who's in Charge of My Life, the Government or Me?

The third warning sign of rising socialism is everyday behavior that's increasingly dictated by the government. It's worth asking yourself, "How much freedom do I forfeit by having to dance to the government's tune every day?"

An incredible number of laws and regulations impinge upon your freedom every day. These include laws and regulations related to:

- wearing seat belts while driving;
- using plastic grocery bags and plastic straws (or not);
- living on a boat;
- sitting or sleeping on sidewalks;
- driving your car, assuming you're allowed to drive;
- riding an electric scooter on a bike path;
- renting out rooms in your house;
- wearing a helmet when on a motorcycle;
- smoking in public places—and sometimes, even in your home.

Most of us eat several times a day, and many of us take medications, which means the U.S. Food & Drug Association is very much involved in our everyday activities. The FDA plays an important role in our health and well-being. A vigilant agency can ensure that the can of tomatoes you take off the grocery store shelf isn't going to contain arsenic, or the blood pressure medication you're taking doesn't contain lead. That being said, the FDA can go overboard sometimes. For example, there are lengthy pizza pie laws, including this amendment to the "Definitions and Standards of Identity or Composition: Elimination of the Pizza Standard," proposed in 2001:

> *The current standard for "Pizza with Meat" requires that the product consist of a bread base with tomato sauce, cheese, and meat topping. The product must contain cooked meat made*

> *from not less than 15 percent raw meat (9 CFR 319.600(a)). The current standard for "Pizza with Sausage" requires that the product consist of a bread base with tomato sauce, cheese, and not less than 12 percent cooked sausage or 10 percent dry sausage (9 CFR 319.600(b)). Thus, if a product subject to FSIS jurisdiction fails to contain any of these components, its labeling cannot bear the term "pizza."*[132]

Hmmmmm. Do we really need the term "pizza" to be so carefully spelled out, complete with definitions and standards of identity? Of course not. (And by the way, how many pizza pies did they have to study to come up with these standards?) This is a classic example of too much government. We're not being safe-guarded in any way. The government should stop wasting our time and money and put its resources into something that makes a difference.

But apparently, the FDA's definition of "something that makes a difference" is a bit loose. In 2019, the agency launched an attempt to prevent the makers of almond milk from using the word "milk" on their products. Why? Because, according to the FDA, only something that comes from "lacteal secretion… obtained by the complete milking of one or more healthy cows" should be called milk.[133] Almonds do not lactate, so they don't qualify as milk.

---

[132] "Definitions and Standards of Identity of Composition: Elimination of the Pizza Standard." *Federal Register*, November 2, 2001. Viewed January 19, 2020. Accessible at https://www.federalregister.gov/documents/2001/11/02/01-27542/definitions-and-standards-of-identity-or-composition-elimination-of-the-pizza-standard.

[133] "The FDA's Fixation on Nut Milk Labeling Is Not About Food Safety or Consumer Health." By Mike Riggs. *Reason*, February 28, 2019. Viewed March 3,

It may just be me, but I think most people old enough to purchase groceries know the difference between almonds and cows. They would not be snookered into buying something labeled "almond milk," thinking it actually came from one or more healthy cows, by way of lacteal secretion.

The "Nanny in Charge"

Not only is the government sometimes regulating our daily lives to the nth degree, it seems to have decided that if we're left to our own devices, we'll destroy ourselves with our foolishness, get our children killed, and end civilization as we know it. In other words, it has appointed itself our collective nanny. Here are some of the ways it is making sure we don't harm ourselves out of our own stupidity:

- In 2012, the city of New York proposed a ban on the sale of sugary drinks in cups larger than 16 ounces, most likely in response to an alarming rise in the rates of obesity. The Board of Health voted unanimously to accept the ban, apparently thinking New Yorkers were too dumb to realize they shouldn't be knocking back that much sugar in one sitting. (Or that they could get around the ban by buying two smaller drinks.) Fortunately, the New York Court of Appeals decided that the Board of Health was "exceeding the scope of its regulatory authority" and repealed the ban in 2015. Whew!

2020. Accessible at https://reason.com/2019/02/28/the-fdas-fixation-on-nut-milk-labeling-i/.

- The city of Fort Lee, New Jersey, passed a law banning texting while jaywalking across the street.[134] Hey, isn't jaywalking already banned in New Jersey? Do they really need to add that texting while committing an act that's banned is also banned? If people are dumb enough to text while jaywalking, they're probably not going to worry about this double-banning.
- The State of Tennessee passed a law regulating how people must wear their pants, apparently to protect the public from getting an eyeful of underwear (or worse) revealed by low-slung pants. It's considered indecent exposure, and Tennessee is pretty strict about it. This headline says it all: "High school students jailed for sagging pants."[135]
- The State of Maryland passed a law saying that camp counselors cannot apply sunscreen to the children's faces and must get parental permission to let any child use sunscreen at camp. The policy also states that, "Under no circumstances should campers assist each other in the application of sunscreen."[136] It seems as if helping out a friend by rubbing sunscreen on his/her back has become a highly dangerous act.

---

[134] "Texting while walking banned in N.J. town." By Chenda Ngak. CBSNews.com, May 15, 2012. Viewed January 19, 2020. Accessible at https://www.cbsnews.com/news/texting-while-walking-banned-in-nj-town/.

[135] "High school students jailed for sagging pants." By Janice Broach and WMCActionNews5.com Staff. WMCActionNews5, December 9, 2015. Viewed May 6, 2020. Accessible at https://www.wmcactionnews5.com/story/30700888/high-school-students-jailed-for-sagging-pants/.

[136] "Md. to require parental permission before kids can use sunscreen." By Marc Fisher. *Washington Post*, January 1, 2011. Viewed January 19, 2020. Accessible at https://www.washingtonpost.com/local/md-to-require-parental-permission-before-kids-can-use-sunscreen/2011/06/30/AGN1AitH_story.html/

- The city Rockville, Maryland, prohibits swearing if a person is on or near a roadway. Plenty of us are offended by the jerks we encounter on the roads, but really: a law against swearing?
- In California, you are not allowed to eat a frog that has died in a frog-jumping contest. Instead, it must be destroyed as soon as possible. Darn! I was looking forward to a free frog legs dinner![137]

It's possible that some of these laws will help make people aware of certain dangers—like not eating frogs that took one leap too many—so they can better protect themselves. But you could accomplish the same thing through public awareness campaigns that highlight the dangers and offer solutions. That's much better than passing these "you're too dumb to take care of yourself" laws that are offensive and so often ineffective.

Where Are We on the Freedom Spectrum?

Ronald Reagan once said that "Government exists to protect us from each other. Where government has gone beyond its limits is in deciding to protect us from ourselves."

If the government truly wants to protect us, let it begin by getting control of the budget, cutting taxes, slashing the countless laws, rules, and regulations that make it difficult to set up and grow a business, and generally unleash American's

[137] "The most ridiculous law in every state." By Melia Robinson and Erin McDowell. *Business Insider*, September 13, 2019. Viewed January 23, 2020. Accessible at https://www.businessinsider.com/weird-state-laws-across-america-2018-1#arkansas-a-pinball-machine-cant-give-away-more-than-25-free-games-to-a-player-who-keeps-winning-the-statute-aims-to-prohibit-machines-that-encourage-gambling-4.

entrepreneurial power. That will make us free, and strong and independent, as Americans should be.

Remember the three ways to gauge where we are on the freedom spectrum? Increases in taxes, enforced contact with the government, and government-dictated behavior. They are all indicators of socialism, and they are all very much on the rise in the United States. We're headed toward the wrong side of the freedom spectrum, and that's a shame because there is no place in the world where happy commies romp through their lives.

Chapter Fifteen

There is No Happy Communism

I grew up in the happiest place on earth!

It must have been the most marvelous place imaginable because everyone in town thronged the streets for the annual May Day parades. Everyone had a job and a place to live, and there was no poverty. We absolutely loved our government, which is why our leaders always received ninety percent or more of the vote—in many cases, no one even bothered running against the people in office, that's how adored they were. The Prime Minister was always cheered when he entered the Federal Assembly. All of his proposals were brilliant and were immediately passed without change.

And it wasn't just in my little part of the communist world that everyone was so happy. It was the same in red country after red country. Or so we were told, as we stood sullenly on the streets or in the parks listening to the holiday speeches. That was the Czechoslovakian attitude toward government: sullen acceptance. In some other communist countries, you couldn't get away with that. Instead, you had to put on a convincing display of "happy communism," or else you might lose your job and home, or be hauled off to jail for a session with the "attitude adjusters." In North Korea, when the "beloved father" died, the people were required to pour into the streets, where they would cry buckets of tears and wail for hours. God help those who did not put a convincing display of grief.

I probably should take back that remark about God because He was frowned upon or even banished in communist paradises. The leaders saw God as an alternative source of guidance and inspiration for the people, and they couldn't allow that. There is only one God allowed in the communist world, and that is communism, as personified by the current leader. Karl Marx, the father of communism, told us that the workers "have nothing to lose but their chains." He was wrong. We had nothing to look forward to but chains, to restrictions on our freedom, opportunities, and happiness.

Does Socialism Work?

Many people today, including major Democratic candidates for the U.S. presidency, claim that socialism *is* good and that it *has* succeeded. They dismiss the undeniable messes and mass murders communism perpetrated in the USSR, China, Venezuela, and other nations. Instead, they point to the Nordic nations. They admire these countries, with Vermont Senator Bernie Sanders saying that "we should look to countries like Denmark, like Sweden and Norway, and learn from what they have accomplished for their working people."[138]

Before we do that, we should note that while these countries are indeed prosperous and offer their citizens a variety of social programs today, and that they were wealthy in the past. But in-between today and the past, they were in dire straits because they had adopted socialism.

[138] "Sen. Warren Reveals Democratic Socialists' Hidden Agenda." By Kerry Jackson. *Investor's Business Daily*, August 17, 2018. Viewed February 7, 2020. Accessible at https://www.investors.com/politics/commentary/warren-democratic-socialist-agenda/.

Sweden, for example, had the 4th highest per capita income in the world in 1970.[139] Then it embraced socialism. The nation's Social Democratic party jacked up taxes, heavily regulated the economy, and set about redistributing resources from the rich to the poor. Swedish socialism "worked" so well that by 1990, the country had dropped from 4th to 14th on the per capita income list. For this and other economic reasons, socialism was pitched. Corporate, property, and capital gains taxes were cut, as was the top income-tax rate. The estate tax and wealth taxes were abolished. Social spending and economic subsidies were reduced significantly, as was the public sector payroll. Government departments that came up with new and costly programs were required to pay for them by cutting something else from their budgetary allotments.

While Sweden was cutting taxes and spending, it was also handing out the incentives. Unemployment payments were reduced, giving people an incentive to work. The nation's postal system lost its monopoly, and the transportation and electricity sectors were deregulated. This allowed for more competition in these areas.

Today, there is no doubt that the Nordic countries have firmly turned their backs on socialism. Sweden, Denmark, Finland, and Norway now "rank among the 30 most capitalist countries in the world."[140] An analysis by Michael Cembalest of J.P. Morgan points out that:

---

[139] "How Sweden Overcame Socialism." By Jesus Fernandez-Villaverde and Lee E. Ohanian. *Wall Street Journal*, January 9, 2019. Viewed February 7, 2020. Accessible at https://www.wsj.com/articles/how-sweden-overcame-socialism-11547078767.

[140] "The Myth of Nordic Socialism." By Rainer Zitelmann. *Barron's*, April 3, 2019. Viewed February 7, 2020. Accessible at https://www.barrons.com/articles/the-myth-of-nordic-socialism-51554296401.

> *...Nordic countries rank even higher than the US with respect to "Business Freedoms", which include streamlined regulations for new businesses creation, and the ease and cost of obtaining licenses and real estate development permits.*[141]

Since turning away from socialism, Sweden's economic growth has outperformed that of the European Union. The nation still has comparatively high taxes and offers programs such as family care and free college education. But remember that the Nordic countries are quite small. Sweden, for example, has only 10 million citizens, which is about the same as the number living in Los Angeles County. Sweden and other Nordic countries have very homogenous populations, which helps promote equality of opportunity, and therefore, equality of income and wealth. Plus—and this is a big plus—they live under the diplomatic and military protection of the United States. As such, they don't have to spend a lot of money on armed forces: Sweden allots only 1.0% of its GDP to military spending, compared to 3.2% for the U.S.[142] This gives them a lot more money to spend on their social programs than they would otherwise have.

It's not just Nordic countries like Sweden that have dropped socialism like a hot potato. Great Britain turned toward socialism following World War II, only to dump it in the 1980s. India and Israel did the same. These countries were lucky because they

---

[141] "Eye on the Market." By Michael Cembalest. J.P. Morgan, June 24, 2019. Page 4. Viewed February 7, 2020. "Accessible at https://www.jpmorgan.com/jpmpdf/1320747403290.pdf.

[142] "Military expenditure (% of GDP)." The World Bank, undated. Viewed February 7, 2020. Accessible at https://data.worldbank.org/indicator/MS.MIL.XPND.GD.ZS.

were allowed to make the choice. In most cases, once a country has gone socialist, it can't escape, not without a revolution.

Be Careful What You Wish For

Despite socialism's horrible track record, a 2019 Gallup Poll[143] showed that young American adults, ages 18-54, feel that socialism is just as enticing as capitalism. They give capitalism a 51% positive rating and socialism a 49% positive rating, which for these types of polls is more or less a tie.

I understand why people in this age range are upset. They may have large college loans to repay and may be priced out of the housing market in several parts of the country. The job market is shaky in many sectors, shrinking to insignificance in others. All the while, newly-minted million and billionaires, awash in cash, are living lives of luxury.

This is happening because capitalism is messy and imperfect. While it has lifted the masses out of poverty in the countries where it has been adopted and offers opportunities for anyone to succeed, it makes no promise that any particular person will do well. The fact that capitalism produces winners and losers is troubling, but not nearly as horrifying as the fact that under communism, there are only losers and losers—unless you're one of the few who rise to leadership, in which case you live like a king.

The truth is that communism can only work—and I use that term loosely because it's always failed—when it keeps everyone tightly controlled. This requires the government

[143] "Socialism as Popular as Capitalism Among Young Adults in U.S." By Lydia Saad. *Gallup*, November 25, 2019. Viewed February 7, 2020. Accessible at https://news.gallup.com/poll/268766/socialism-popular-capitalism-among-young-adults.aspx.

to take away the people's freedom, and that runs counter to human instincts. We were born to be free. We were born to desire more for ourselves and our families. We were born to strive, to respond to incentives and opportunities by working harder or better, by trying something different and by inventing something entirely new. Yes, there's an element of greed in all this, and yes, there's a willingness to place your desires above those of others. But that's what we human beings are. Capitalism is built on this understanding. On the recognition of what makes us tick, what gets us to work harder and better. That's why communism cannot work, has never and will never work. It just doesn't "get" us.

It does get a lot of attention with its enticing promises, but it does not understand who we are. So it resorts to threats. To force. To evicting people from their houses and taking away their jobs. To telling them that they are bad for wanting or having more than others. To building walls to keep it's "happy comrades" in, and to shooting them as they attempt to crawl over the barbed wire atop those walls to freedom.

If socialism creates a workers' paradise where everyone is happy and well-cared for, why do so many people risk everything to escape it? Because they crave opportunity. Even more than that, they want freedom. Freedom, with all its responsibilities and with the built-in fear of failure, is always more enticing than the fetters of communism.

That's because it is only with freedom that we can soar.

It's All About Carrying Your Own Weight

Communism is the opposite of freedom, in every way. Under communism, you don't have the freedom to think and worship as you wish, to live where you want, or to plan your future as you see fit. You don't have the freedom to criticize the government or, God forbid, try to change things. You don't even have the freedom to try to make a better life for yourself, for you have to have special permission to earn more money, if such a thing is even allowed in your country.

As soon as I stepped off the plane in New York in 1988, I felt as if I was in a nation where people had all these freedoms. And just as importantly, they had the freedom to fail. I didn't understand this when I arrived in America, for I was only nineteen, but I came to realize that being free to fail is an essential part of genuine freedom, for it is only when you are free to fail that you can truly soar.

This can be a difficult concept to understand. After all, who doesn't want to be protected against failure? Who enjoys being wrong, possibly losing their job or status, and all their money? Doesn't it make sense that you would be more successful if someone was constantly watching and telling you what to do?

It makes sense when we're babies and children, with our parents helping us take our first steps, guiding our hands as we learn how to write, coaching us at sports, and teaching us to be good people. Our parents have our best interests at heart, so they gradually encourage us to take more and more responsibility for ourselves. Unfortunately, the communist government is not this loving parent. Instead, it is the greedy parent that wants more and more control. It is the nanny parent that feels it knows more than you do. It is the forever parent that wants to keep control over you until the end. And it is the uncaring parent that really has no interest in you. You're just a number to the various levels of government, a birth number and a driver's license number, a Communist Party number and a professional certification number, a this number and a that number. If we can truly call a communist government a parent at all, it's one in the form of a giant orphanage with so many kids to care for that they don't even want to know your name.

Communism is truly the parent that doesn't want to know your name. It just wants you to do and think what you're supposed to so the orphanage will keep running, will keep producing enough profit to keep the "parents" living in grand style. You can think of communism as one of those awful orphans' houses in a Charles Dickenson novel, where the children are fed barely enough and made to work hard all day long, while the governors sit down to gorge themselves on expensive foods, dressed in the latest and finest styles.

I spent my early life in this communist's orphan's workhouse. I know, first hand, how miserable life is with this greedy, forever, uncaring, parent.

That's why we must insist on being free from government control as much as possible, which means we must be willing to take as much responsibility for our own lives as possible. And that, of course, means we must embrace the freedom to fail. And we *will* fail, all of us, at one point or another—maybe many times, in many ways. But it's only through failure that we become stronger, wiser, and better equipped to succeed next time. As Eleanor Roosevelt said, "Freedom makes a huge requirement of every human being. With freedom comes responsibility. For the person who is unwilling to grow up, the person who does not want to carry his own weight, this is a frightening prospect."

It's true, carrying your own weight can be frightening. I remember the fear I felt the first time I went up in an airplane to skydive. My father had to push me out the door. I had been trained, I knew I could do it, but was too frightened to take the plunge. So he made me grow up, right then and there. Since then, I have happily jumped out of a plane many times and absolutely love sky diving.

I was also terribly frightened when planning to leave Czechoslovakia. I had told way too many people what I was planning to do, which was a very risky thing to do in a country where informers were everywhere. Was I subconsciously hoping that I would be caught? Perhaps. But I faced my fears. I risked being caught by the Czechoslovakian secret police. I "carried my own weight" and was rewarded by being allowed to live in, and later become a citizen of, the United States.

I scored some of my greatest successes when risking failure, and I'm not alone. America's Founding Fathers knew there was a good chance their rebellion would be crushed and they would hang from the highest tree. But they saw the struggle through and created this wonderful country. In Czechoslovakia, people like Vaclav Havel stood up to the communists, suffering through years in prison before becoming the first president of the free state of Czechoslovakia in 1989. In Poland, Lech Walesa risked everything facing down the communists, as did the thousands of Eastern Europeans who protested against communism, crawled under barbed wire and through sewers to escape their masters, and took sledge hammers to the Berlin Wall, finally toppling the hated system.

It's impossible to calculate how much these and millions of other people have done for themselves, their families, their countries, and the world. And they did it, as Eleanor Roosevelt said, by being willing to carry their own weight.

That is what communism does not want you to do. But it is the essence of liberty.

We *must* carry our own weight, for when the government carries it for us, we lose our freedom. And without freedom, we have nothing.

President Dwight Eisenhower once said: “If all that Americans want is security, they can go to prison. They’ll have enough to eat, a bed and a roof over their heads. But if an American wants to preserve his dignity and his equality as a human being, he must not bow his neck to any dictatorial government.”

In other words, there is no commie paradise. Communist, socialist, democratic socialist: whatever it calls itself, this type of government is always a disaster. Its promises may seem enticing, but once you’re in its grip, the only way out is over the barbed wire.

Chapter Sixteen

Loving the U.S.A.

Our calendar is full of holidays and days of commemoration. There's the 4th of July, Memorial Day, Martin Luther King Day, Christmas, Passover, Ramadan, Thanksgiving, Flag Day, Groundhog Day, and many more. But there's one day of remembrance that most of us have never celebrated, and possibly never even heard of: Bill of Rights Day.

December 15, 1941, was the 150th anniversary of the day the State of Virginia ratified the Bill of Rights, otherwise known as the first ten amendments to the Constitution. That made Virginia the tenth of the then fourteen U.S. states to approve it, completing the necessary three-quarters of states needed to confirm the Bill of Rights as part of our foundational law. In 1941, President Franklin Roosevelt proclaimed December 15 as Bill of Rights Day. On that day, President Roosevelt declared that people all over the nation should fly the flag and think about the significance of the first ten amendments to our Constitution, noting in his radio address, "No date in the long history of freedom means more to liberty-loving men in all liberty-loving countries than the fifteenth day of December 1791."[144]

However, because Japan had bombed Pearl Harbor just a week before this commemoration, celebrations of Bill of Rights Day were lost in the shuffle as people prepared for world war.

---

[144] "Bill of Rights Day explained." By Ashley Novak. *CNN*, updated December 15, 2019. Viewed March 31, 2020. Accessible at https://www.cnn.com/2019/12/15/us/bill-of-rights-day-explained-trnd/index.html.

Thus, it wasn't until 1946 that another proclamation, this one issued by President Harry Truman, designated December 15 of that year as Bill of Rights Day. Since 1962, all of our presidents have faithfully issued the same proclamation annually.

The Bill of Rights was created to enumerate and enshrine some of the most basic rights of the people. While the Constitution describes the composition and duties of the federal government and the rights of the states, the Bill of Rights was designed to be a guarantee of liberty for the people. As the Library of Congress explains:

> *The First Amendment guarantees freedom of religion, speech, and the press, and the rights of peaceful assembly and petition. Other amendments guarantee the rights of the people to form a "well-regulated militia," to keep and bear arms, the rights to private property, fair treatment for accused criminals, protection from unreasonable search and seizure, freedom from self-incrimination, a speedy and impartial jury trial, and representation by counsel.*[145]

Our Founding Fathers believed that the people actually had many more rights, apart from those mentioned in the Bill of Rights. But between the Bill of Rights, the limited nature of the federal government as described in the Constitution, and the rights guaranteed to the people in most state constitutions, they believed freedom for the people would be guaranteed.

Notice that neither the Constitution nor the Bill of Rights said anything about the government giving these and other

[145] "Today in History – December 15: The Bill of Rights." Library of Congress, document undated. Viewed March 30, 2020. Accessible at https://www.loc.gov/item/today-in-history/december-15/.

rights to the people. That's because our founders understood that such rights were inalienable, granted in perpetuity to the people by the Almighty. They believed it was the duty of the government to protect these God-given rights. As John Adams said: "Liberty must at all hazards be supported. We have a right to it, derived from our Maker." Thomas Jefferson added:

> *Under the law of nature, all men are born free, every one [sic] comes into the world with a right to his own person, which includes the liberty of moving and using it at his own will. This is what is called personal liberty, and is given him by the author of nature...*[146]

But even as our Founding Fathers created a government dedicated to preserving our God-given rights to life and liberty, they feared what would happen if the people forgot where their rights came from and failed to protect their liberty diligently against government encroachment. And therein lies the problem for us today! We, as a nation, are no longer taught to understand the nature of our rights, and to realize that we must continually fight to preserve them. To know that one of the greatest threats to our liberty is ignorance of our rights, and an ever-growing reliance on government for help. It's no wonder that our rights have been severely eroded.

[146] "Primary Resource: Thomas Jefferson's Argument in *Howell v. Netherland* (1700)." Encyclopedia Virginia, entry last modified February 6, 2014. Viewed April 7, 2020. Accessible at https://www.encyclopediavirginia.org/thomas_jefferson_s_argument_in_howell_v_netherland_1770.

Here We Go Again!

Our rights have long been under attack. Sometimes the threat arises from genuine disagreement over issues, or questions about how to apply a document that was ratified in 1791 to modern times. After all, no one back then imagined there would be such things as Facebook and pizza-delivering drones, or that terrorists would stuff explosives in their underwear and shoes and attempt to destroy airplanes at 30,000 feet up in the sky.

Much of the time, however, our rights are assailed by interest groups hoping to erase long-established rights—such as the right to own guns—or create new "rights" where none have existed. On such imaginary "right" is government-mandated insurance coverage for contraception and abortions.

Then there are those who would like to sweep away many of our rights in favor of new ones our Founders never contemplated—because these "rights" would require the government to take on frightening power. In essence, they want to turn the meaning of the Bill of Rights on its head, and the idea of American liberty along with it. You can see this quite clearly in Senator Bernie Sanders' "21st Century Economic Bill of Rights." In a speech titled "Democratic Socialism," Sanders conceded that the Bill of Rights protects our liberty and that the essence of that liberty is freedom from "authoritarian tyranny." But then he said that we must:

> *...guarantee every man, woman and child in our country basic economic rights – the right to quality health care, the right to as much education as one needs to succeed in our society, the right to a good job that pays a living wage, the right to affordable housing, the right*

> *to a secure retirement, and the right to live in a clean environment.*

Note that Sanders is calling for these to be *guaranteed rights*, promised and delivered by the government, an idea that turns the meaning of the Bill of Rights on its head. Our Founders wanted very much to keep the government off the peoples' backs. But Sanders wants the opposite, to affix the government to our backs forever. This would turn our government from a sentinel fiercely protecting our liberty into a mother/mugger who with one hand would shower us with "free" goodies, and with the other steal our money to pay for it all.

But there are no free goodies! There never have been and never will be. Remember: the government does not have money of its own to hand out; it does not *earn* money, it *takes* money. It takes money from us. And every time it does, it takes away a bit of our liberty. This is necessary to a certain degree. A well-funded government can protect our shores from invading armies, build highways and other infrastructure, and run the courts that help us settle our disputes and put criminals in jail. But once it moves beyond these essential functions, we have to wrestle with trade-offs, such as:

- How much government expansion are we willing to tolerate?
- How much more freedom are we willing to surrender in exchange for goodies?
- How much are we willing to move from voluntarily giving the government money for limited purposes, to being forced to surrender it for unlimited purposes?
- How much decision-making do we want to hold on to, and how much are we willing to hand over to the government?

- How much do we trust the government to honor its promises and choose the right course for us in each and every situation?

If Senator Sanders has his way, we will all be forced to surrender our money, our will, and our freedom to a very powerful and pervasive government. We will have no choice because a government that delivers all these goodies must dominate or totally control our nation's health and education sectors, housing and job markets, and more. It will be required to give a well-paying job to everyone who wants one and will sometimes force businesses to hire these people, whether they are needed or not. Once they're hired, it won't matter whether these people work hard or spend the day playing online solitaire, for they will be on the payroll, forever. How can this possibly benefit the nation? It can't, of course. But all of us will be required to contribute to these salaries. And all of us will suffer if and when these employees neglect of their duties.

The simple truth is that the government cannot guarantee liberty while at the same time guaranteeing an endless supply of "free" goodies for everyone. These two things cannot be granted by a single source. The only approach that really works is a government that focuses on protecting liberty, while allowing the free market to flourish, creating wealth and plenty for all.

Sanders, Roosevelt & Ocasio-Cortez

Senator Sanders makes no bones about his love for socialism, and his ideas have attracted a lot of attention. Yet they are nothing new. Back in 1944, President Franklin Roosevelt presented his idea for a "second Bill of Rights."[147] These rights included:

> *"The right to a useful and remunerative job [...]*
>
> *"The right to earn enough to provide adequate food and clothing and recreation;*
>
> *"The right of every farmer to raise and sell his products at a return which will give him and his family a decent living [...]*
>
> *"The right of every family to a decent home;*
>
> *"The right to adequate medical care [...]*
>
> *"The right to adequate protection from the economic fears of old age [...]*
>
> *"The right to a good education [...]"*

Sound familiar? President Roosevelt went on to ask Congress "to explore the means for implementing this economic bill of rights- for it is definitely the responsibility of the Congress so to do." In other words, Roosevelt believed it was the government's responsibility to provide goodies for the people.

The connection between Roosevelt's "second Bill of Rights" and Sanders' "21st Century Economic Bill of Rights" is clear and direct. We can see similar attitudes and beliefs in other public figures, including Representative Alexandria

---

[147] "State of the Union Message to Congress, January 11, 1944." By Franklyn Roosevelt. Franklin D. Roosevelt Presidential Library and Museum. Viewed April 2, 2020. Accessible at http://www.fdrlibrary.marist.edu/archives/address text.html.

Ocasio-Cortez, the young congresswoman from New York. In 2019, Ocasio-Cortez teamed with Senator Edward Markey of Massachusetts to propose the "Green New Deal" [148] resolution to Congress, a bill that supposedly protected the environment but concluded with a call for:

> *"(H) guaranteeing a job with a family-sustaining wage, adequate family and medical leave, paid vacations, and retirement security to all people of the United States; ...*
>
> *"(O) providing all people of the United States with—*
>
> *(i) high-quality health care;*
> *(ii) affordable, safe, and adequate housing;*
> *(iii) economic security; and*
> *(iv) clean water, clean air, healthy and affordable food, and access to nature."*

Guaranteed jobs, guaranteed houses and high-quality health care, economic security, all under the guise of protecting the environment. From Roosevelt in the 1930s, to Sanders, to Ocasio-Cortez, who may still be in office forty or fifty years from now. The language changes, but the intent is the same: flip the Bill of Rights on its head. Change the government from being the protector of our liberty to the bestower of endless goodies, who must, of course, rob us of our liberty and cash in order to provide these "freebies" to everyone.

Am I exaggerating? Am I seeing links to socialism where none exist? Not according to the Communist Party USA,

---

[148] "H. Res. 109 – Recognizing the duty of the Federal Government to create a Green New Deal." Congress.gov. Viewed April 2, 2020. Accessible at https://www.congress.gov/bill/116th-congress/house-resolution/109/text.

which includes this paragraph on a page titled "Bill of Rights Socialism"[149] on its website:

> *Socialism in the United States would be built on the strong foundation of our Constitution's Bill of Rights... The rights to a job, to health care, and education must also be guaranteed by the Constitution.*

Guaranteed jobs, education, health care: the line connecting Roosevelt to Sanders to Ocasio-Cortez is firmly anchored to the Communist Party USA. So I'm not exaggerating. Clearly, the American dream of individual liberty, freedom from heavy-handed government, and the right to live life on your own terms is, and long has been, under assault.

Remember December 15th!

The best way to protect ourselves and our freedom is to return to the Bill of Rights, our Founder's ideal of a government that is the protector of liberty. There's no particular law that needs to be passed to achieve this, no 800-page congressional resolution that will accomplish this recapturing of our rights. We must, instead, begin by changing our attitudes.

Whenever trouble arises and someone cries, "There ought to be a law about this," we should answer, "We don't need another law." There are so many laws, rules, and regulations already on the books that experts can't even count them.

---

[149] "Bill of Rights Socialism." By Robert Wood and Dee Miles. Communist Party USA, May 1, 2016, Viewed April 2, 2020. Accessible at https://www.cpusa.org/party_info/socialism-in-the-usa/.

When someone shouts, "This country is evil," we should answer, "This is the greatest country the world has ever seen. Yes, we have made mistakes. But we have long been, and remain, a beacon of freedom, opportunity, and prosperity to the world."

When someone insists, "I demand a safe space where only people like me are allowed," we should answer, "That's segregation, that's discrimination, that's exactly what we've been fighting against for decades."

When someone yells, "You've microaggressed me, you should be ashamed," we should answer, "Grow up."

When someone complains, "They're not teaching public school in my native language," we should answer, "You came to this country voluntarily. It's up to you to learn our language and customs."

When someone whines, "I want the government to give me more," we should ask, "What have you contributed to the country?"

When someone asserts, "We need a new bill of rights," we should answer, "The original one is exactly right."

We must revise our priorities, putting liberty above comfort, restraining the urge to cast aside freedom in exchange for freebies or a quick fix at the slightest sign of distress.

We must restrict government, which by nature continually seeks to expand, because the greater its power grows, the less freedom we enjoy.

We must revere our nation, its history and people. Although our founders were imperfect, and so is the country they created, we have come closer than any other nation to the goal of shared liberty and prosperity, and are continuing to move forward.

We must restore the Bill of Rights to the place of honor it once held in our hearts and heads. We must return to its ideals in order to live life as truly free people.

I Love the USA!

To sum it all up, we must learn to cherish our God-given rights and freedom, as our founders did.

We must rediscover the strength and fortitude we have within, as they did when challenging the mightiest military power then in existence.

We must remember that our nation draws power from unity, not from dividing ourselves into a multitude of warring political, ethnic, religious, and other groups.

We must remind ourselves that while the government has a vital role to play, the best government is small, lean, and treads lightly on our liberty.

It was this promise of liberty that got me to flee communist Czechoslovakia and come to this country, a nineteen-year-old girl who knew nothing about American save that it was the land of liberty.

From the first moment on, I made every effort to assimilate. I didn't expect anyone to support me, so I got a job right away. I dove headfirst into learning the language and mastering the customs, and even changed my name from Jana Kandlova to Jane Benson. Not because I had to, but because I wanted to. I didn't want America to change to fit me, I wanted to fit myself into the land of freedom and opportunity.

I renounced my Czechoslovakian citizenship, which felt like cutting my own umbilical cord. After all, I loved the land and people of my birth, and I loved the family I left behind. But

I desperately wanted to be American, and I have never regretted my decision. I can proudly say that I love the U.S.A.!

I love our freedom.

I love the daring-do that lets us do things like send astronauts to the moon and invent the internet.

I love our freedom to decide how to live our lives. You can wake up this morning and decide to alter the course of your life—and many do.

I love the spirit of adventure that drives people to dream of creating new businesses, charities, art groups, and other things—and then doing so.

I love our refusal to back down, to push through terrible times like the Great Depression and create new, better times.

I love the fact that we can worship God any way we choose—or not worship at all.

I love the fact that we are a very generous nation, opening our hearts and wallets to people in need in this country and abroad.

I love our diversity, with people from all over the world contributing their ideas and energy.

I love the U.S. because it went toe-to-toe with Nazism and Communism, and is now standing up to radical Islamicists who wish to shove the world back into the 10th century.

I love this country for the capitalism which lifted our standard of living higher than our ancestors could possibly have imagined, and which has spread around the world to bring new life and possibilities to everyone.

I love this country for its democracy.

And I love the inspiration we can draw from our Founding Fathers, who pledged to each other "our Lives, our Fortunes, and our sacred Honor" in their quest for liberty.

President Kennedy asked us to think about what we can do for our country. Perhaps the best thing is to pledge ourselves to the continual quest for liberty—true liberty, as our Founders understood liberty.

1993- Celebrating
my Green Card

1975-
My Father, Mother, myself and
baby sister, Eva

Approximately 1977-78-
the Little Stars of Communism
being indoctrinated

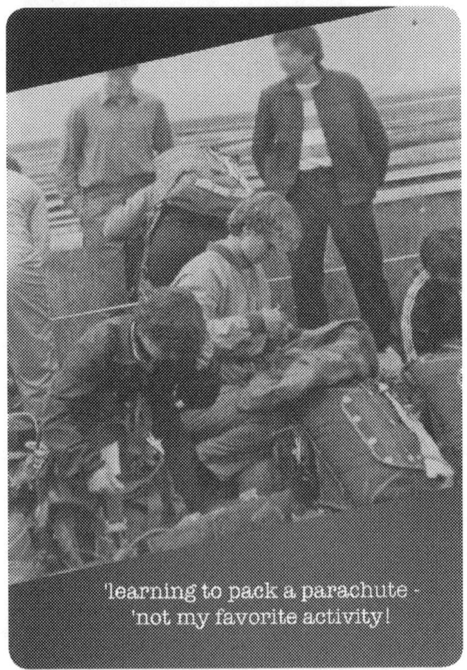

'learning to pack a parachute -
'not my favorite activity!

1966 My Mom & Dad

1984- My Father was a Sky Diver and I thought I'd try something a little adventurous, too; unaware, however, that the best were being singled out for the Military.
I was selected

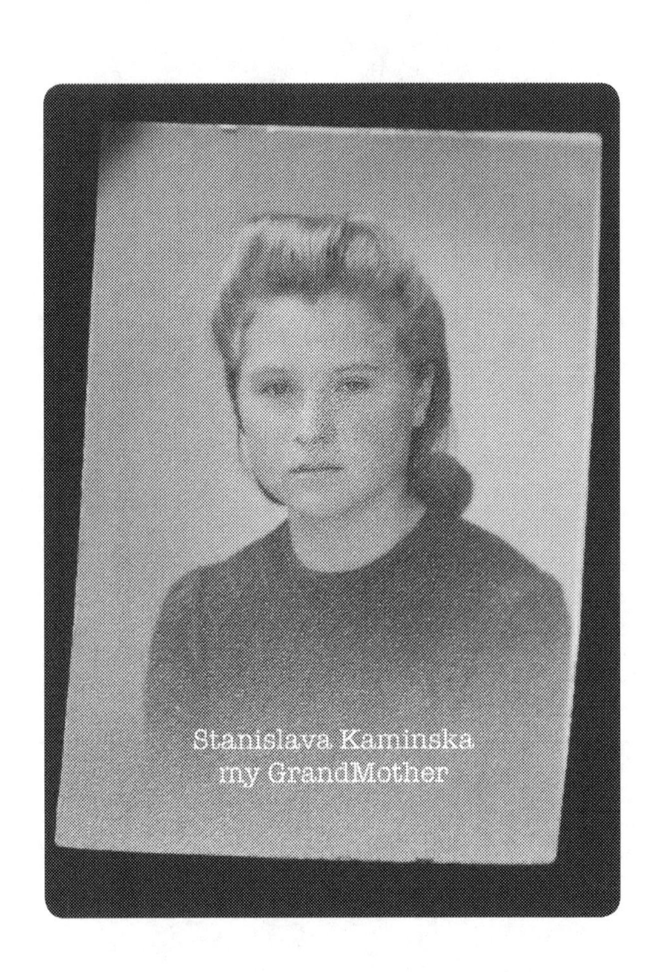

Stanislava Kaminska
my GrandMother

Epilogue

It was July 4th, 1988, when I, Jana Kandlova, escaped communism and came to America. Now I, Jane Benson, watch in dismay as our liberty fades away.

Just as in communist-ruled countries, our freedoms are being tampered with and taken away. Little by little, we are being systematically stripped of our God-given rights. Our "city on a hill" is slowly sliding down into a bottomless government swamp.

As I learned from Rush Limbaugh and Jim Vicevich, if you want to keep God-given rights, you must stand up for them. I didn't understand this at first. I thought our rights were guaranteed by the government. As it turns out, we the people have to fight for them, for government is on the march, driven by an unquenchable thirst for power.

I wrote this book because our quest begins with awareness. I hope that you will now educate and inspire others, and we can energize the light of liberty that makes America a beacon of freedom and hope to the world.

Printed in the United States
By Bookmasters